ABOUT THE AUTHOR

Leslie Bendaly, speaker, workshop leader, and bestselling author, challenges and inspires organizations, teams and individuals to tap the best of themselves and provides them with the tools they need to realize their goals.

She is a North American leader in the fields of teamwork, group processes, synergistics and peak performance management in environments of change. Leslie is seen as a pioneer in the development of tools and systems for increasing synergy and exceptional performance within teams and across organizations as well as in identifying trends with which individuals and their organizations must be in tune if they are to continue to thrive. Her tools and concepts have been developed and tested through her work with hundreds of organizations from large multinationals such as IBM and Warner Lambert to government and small community organizations.

Leslie also designs and facilitates off site events for teams and organizations, team processes and interventions, such as new team kick offs, team development and planning sessions. She heads Ortran, a consulting firm dedicated to providing individuals, teams and organizations with the inspiration and tools to achieve in environments of hyper-change.

Her other books include *Strength in Numbers*, *Games Teams Play*, *More Games Teams Play*, *Organization 2000*, *Winner Instinct*, *The Facilitation Skills Training Kit*, and *Brain Teasers for Team Leaders*. Leslie's work is recognized in *Who's Who in Canada*, *Who's Who in Canadian Business*, and *Who's Who of Canadian Women*.

She is based in Toronto.

VISIT LESLIE AT HER WEBSITE: www.lbendaly.com

*Dedicated to Jacqueline Brougham who
had the remarkable ability to bring out
the best in individuals and teams by
giving the very best of herself.*

ON TRACK

TAKING MEETINGS FROM GOOD TO
GREAT

Leslie Bendaly

 **McGraw-Hill Ryerson**

Toronto   Montréal   Boston   Burr Ridge, IL   Dubuque, IA   Madison, WI   New York
San Francisco   St. Louis   Bangkok   Bogotá Caracas   Kuala Lumpur   Lisbon   London   Madrid
Mexico City   Milan   New Delhi   Santiago   Seoul   Singapore   Sydney   Taipei

McGraw-Hill
Ryerson Limited

A Subsidiary of The **McGraw·Hill** Companies

ISBN: 0-07-089309-8

1234567890 MP 098765432
Printed and bound in Canada.

National Library of Canada Cataloguing in Publication Data

Bendaly, Leslie
    On Track: taking meetings from good to great

Includes index.
ISBN 0-07-089309-8

1. Meetings. I. Title.

HF5734.5.B46 2001   658.4'56   C2001-902308-1

Publisher: **Joan Homewood**
Editorial Co-ordinator: **Catherine Leek**
Production Co-ordinator: **Nicla Dattolico**
Editor: **Tita Zierer**
Electronic Page Composition: **Jay Tee Graphics**
Interior and Cover Design: **Sharon Lucas**
Cover Image: © **Nip Rogers/The Stock Illustration Source**

TABLE OF CONTENTS

Introduction

Imagine being asked to develop your company's Web site or prepare the annual financial report with no training whatsoever. It sounds ludicrous, doesn't it? And yet it is common practice to arm individuals with no more than a flip chart and markers (or laptop and projector, if you have updated meeting facilities) and to expect them to facilitate meetings, the outcomes of which directly impact the success of the team and organization.

Leading effective meetings can be an incredibly challenging task. After all, what could require more know-how than the act of bringing together a group of individuals with different styles, needs, experiences and perspectives and creating an energetic dialogue among them that leads to exceptional outcomes?

In today's team-based business environment, most decisions are made, sold and delivered through meetings of one sort or another. It may be a group of people who come together in a "one-time" meeting, a formal meeting of a team that works together on an ongoing basis, a quick team huddle or a *tête-à-tête* between two people. When these meetings are skillfully facilitated, the outcomes are superior decisions, accompanied by full understanding of the decision, buy-in and effective implementation.

Not surprisingly then, meeting facilitation has been called **the** core competency of the 21st Century. It is the "soft" skill most directly linked to the success of the team and organization.

The effectiveness of a company's meetings reflects the long-term effectiveness of the organization. Employees with strong meeting facilitation skills are increasingly being recognized for the value they bring to their organization, while those without these skills are at a disadvantage.

The good news is that it is not difficult to learn how to use the tools that can increase the effectiveness of your meetings. Whether you lead meetings as an outside facilitator or as a group member who has been asked to step in and lead the group's meetings, the tools and tips provided in *On Track* will help you achieve greater meeting success with ease.

It will provide you with the tools to prepare for and run meetings that will keep your group focused on the objective, ensure full and productive participation, spark innovative thinking, reach outstanding decisions and generate the buy-in required for success. The Meeting Map is your guide and planning tool. It ensures you include all the factors essential to meeting success. The problem-solving and decision-making tools provide the structure and encourage the objectivity required for superior decisions and consensus. In addition *On Track* is full of tips and methods for handling almost any meeting facilitation challenge including dealing with conflict, getting members to take ownership for the success of the meeting and facilitating meetings in which senior peoples' behavior may negatively affect the process.

If you are just beginning as a meeting facilitator, *On Track* provides all of the basics you need to get started. If you are currently leading meetings and feeling frustrated by the group's inability to work together effectively to get the quality results they need, *On Track* will give you the knowledge you need to facilitate high energy, focused meetings in which full and productive participation ensures the group meets its objectives efficiently and effectively. Or, if you are a seasoned facilitator, *On Track* will provide the knowledge and tools that help take your already good meetings to an even higher level of success.

THE ROLE OF THE FACILITATOR

Everyone knows when they have been to a good meeting. You feel like the time was used effectively, you were engaged and you often feel invigorated. When you have been to a "bad" meeting, you also have very specific feelings – that you wasted time, that the decisions were not good or will not work. You may feel a high level of frustration.

The quality of the meeting experience is determined by the skill level of the meeting facilitator.

The Meeting Facilitator

A facilitator is an individual who creates the environment and provides the tools and structure that support others in getting their jobs done and achieving their goals.

The meeting facilitator is responsible for the quality of the group process, ensuring members interact in such a way as to achieve superior performance. That means the way members work together in the meeting is highly effective and the outcomes they achieve are of the highest quality.

In the traditional definition of the meeting facilitator, the facilitator focuses only on the process. The facilitator is the group process expert and does not become involved in the content of the meeting or task of the group. Facilitators, based on the traditional definition, do not have a stake in the results of the meeting and are not content experts. In *On Track* we refer to these meeting leaders as *outside facilitators*. They may be professional facilitators contracted from outside the organization or skilled professionals from within the organization who are not members of the group that is meeting and do not have a stake in the decisions or outcomes. The outside facilitator's biggest challenges come from unfamiliarity with the group members and the nuances of the group's interaction. The outside facilitator must spend time upfront meeting with the team leader and other members to better understand the dynamics of the group and their organization.

A large percentage of meetings, however, are led by the leaders or members of the group that is meeting. These individuals have the challenge of facilitating the meeting in a way that ensures a positive group process with open dialogue and at the same time contributing to the discussion and decisions. We refer to these meeting leaders as *inside facilitators*. Achieving this balance of roles is the biggest challenge for the inside facilitator.

Throughout *On Track* we also refer to "team leaders." The "team leader" refers to the person who is responsible for an

YOUR NOTES

intact team. This could be any work group whose members have a common goal perhaps a department or a project team. In all likelihood, they will be the person deciding whether an outside facilitator is required for the meeting. If they determine an outside facilitator is not necessary, they may take the role of meeting facilitator too as discussed above.

Types of Meetings

Just as there are different types of facilitators, there are different types of meetings. There are two basic types that we refer to:

The *regular team* (or operational) meeting is a meeting held frequently, from daily to monthly, depending on the team and their mandate. These meetings are relatively short, usually approximately an hour in length, but, depending on frequency, may range from one-half to three hours. Most often these meetings have several agenda items. The meetings may be information-sharing meetings or decision-making meetings or a mix of both. These meetings are usually led by an inside facilitator, a team leader or other member of the group.

The *focused group process* is a meeting held to address a particular need. The meeting could be a problem-solving, strategic planning, or team building session. This type of meeting is longer in length, usually from a half day to two days or more. These may be meetings of intact teams or may be made up of members who have no goals in common outside of this particular meeting. These meetings are best led by an outside facilitator.

The Facilitator's Challenge

On Track was inspired by the questions received from meeting facilitators at workshops and newsletter subscribers looking for answers to their most common challenges. Here are a few of them:

- I've had quite a bit of experience facilitating meetings and don't do too badly but an important one is coming up. I will be leading a half day meeting in which a cross-functional group of about 25 people will be making some important decisions about a new product launch. Here are my concerns:

  1. The V.P. of our division will be there. He voices his opinions strongly. How can I prevent him from taking over?

2. One or two others are unhappy campers and will be negative in the meeting in spite of the V.P.'s presence.

3. How do I get full participation and consensus from 25 people in a relatively short time?

- Help please! My manager has just asked me to facilitate our next team meeting. I've never led a meeting before and, on top of that, the main agenda item is something quite contentious that we are supposed to make a decision on. I'm terrified but don't think it would be good for my career if I pass. Any really quick tips?

- I recently led a decision-making meeting that I thought had been very successful. There was quite a bit of discussion and some very enthusiastic participants. We came to a decision that everyone agreed to. Now we have some people who don't appear to be fully supportive and implementation of the decision isn't going well. I'd like to blame those who now aren't supportive but I have a feeling that I must have missed something in the meeting. Any thoughts?

These people are looking for quick answers. Facilitation skills are built over time through learning and practice. But there are a multitude of tools and tips that you can pick and choose from that can immediately increase the effectiveness of meetings. That is what *On Track* is all about.

Do you identify with any of the concerns described in the questions above? Are there others that you would add? Considering specifically what you would like to learn can help you use *On Track* more effectively. The Personal Guide to *On Track* (Figure A) is provided to help you use *On Track* as a personal development tool.

GETTING THE MOST FROM *On Track*

Most knowledge shared in *On Track* applies to any meeting situation. However, if you are looking for quick tips to deal with some specific meeting challenges, check The Quick Guide to Better Meetings (Figure B).

If you lead regular team meetings for your group you will find something of importance in every chapter of *On Track* but if you are skimming the book for nuggets be sure to check the following sections of *On Track*:

YOUR NOTES

Figure A: Personal Guide to *On Track*

List your facilitation questions below. When you come across an answer record the name of the tool, tip or technique and the page number.

How do you?	Tool, tip, technique	*On Track* Page Number

Figure B: The Quick Guide to Better Meetings

The Tips

Throughout *On Track* you will find shaded boxes with different icons to provide some quick advice. These tips are identifiable by their different icons.

Try This

These tips are ideas you might try out that will help you more effectively deal with a particular situation or take your meeting to a higher level.

Caution

These tips describe common situations that can occur to hinder the effectiveness of a meeting.

Handle with Care

These tips warn facilitators of common impending problems. Facilitators will need to take special care in these situations so that a problem does not develop or escalate.

YOUR NOTES

We start with The Meeting Map that describes each step on route to exceptional meeting experiences.
Enjoy!

Chapter 1

The Meeting Map

The destination that most meeting leaders aim for is exceptional outcomes or decisions that are supported with the commitment required to see them effectively implemented. Carefully following The Meeting Map, as outlined in Figure 1-1, greatly increases the likelihood of reaching those results. Meeting leaders tell me the map is critical to their success. When they follow it they lead highly successful meetings. When they forget the map, or even a step in the map, things go less smoothly.

The map is a guide for you, the facilitator. It describes the steps that ensure a successful meeting. It is also a planning tool as you should think about each of the steps in your preparation.

When leading a focused group process such as a problem-solving, team building, brainstorming session, or focus group, you will benefit from following the map closely. When leading regular team or operational meetings, you will benefit from understanding the map and selecting the steps that are most important for that particular meeting. Using the Map for a regular meeting is discussed at the end of this chapter (page 52).

Some steps in the Map are relatively time-consuming and require particular tools; others are short and extremely simple. In fact, some are so simple they may be overlooked as unimportant. When your goal is as complex as getting a group of people to work together extremely well, everything is important. The smallest and simplest steps can make the greatest difference.

Figure 1.1: The Meeting Map

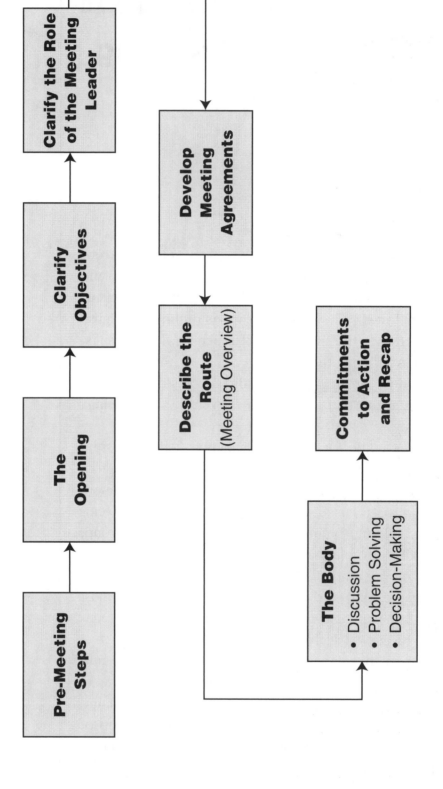

PRE-MEETING STEPS

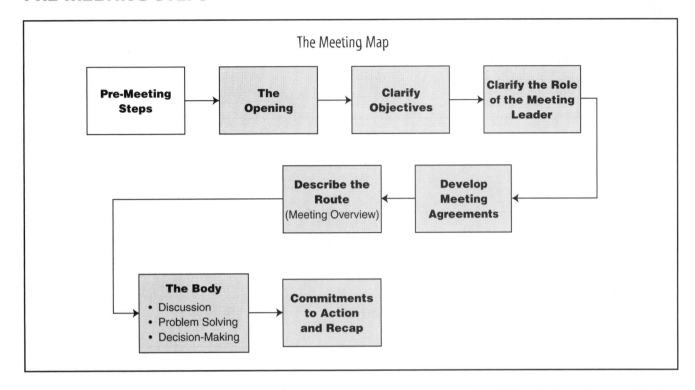

The Meeting Map

The success of a meeting and the quality of the decisions that come out of it depend very much on the preparation work that has been done. This includes planning and agenda setting, inviting the right people, liaising with the team's leader or sponsor, information gathering, defining roles and choosing the best venue or meeting room. As the individual facilitating the meeting, you will not always manage or have direct control over each of these but you should be aware of what is happening in each of these areas and influence them as necessary. Poor preparation can greatly handicap a meeting and set you up for potential failure or at the very least an up-hill battle. Use the Pre-Meeting Steps Checklist (Figure 1-2) to check that you have covered all six steps.

The impact of poor planning can be multifold. A few examples follow.

A meeting invitation or announcement that presents poorly described objectives can create the wrong expectations. Poorly described objectives can result in misunderstanding and misperceptions creating scenarios such as people arriving ready for an argument or with unrealistic expectations of what the group can actually accomplish in the allotted time. A strong facilitator

YOUR NOTES

Figure 1.2: Pre-Meeting Steps Checklist

Meeting Objective

I fully understand the objective. ☐

_____

_____

The wording is clear. ☐

_____

_____

The objective is realistic. ☐
i.e. • sufficient time
• participants have the required knowledge/skills/authority

_____

_____

The Right Participants

Is any one (any skill/knowledge) missing? ☐

_____

_____

Is there a rationale for including each meeting member? ☐
i.e. each person has something to contribute or something to gain by being there.

_____

_____

Learning About the Group

For Outside Facilitators
Meet with the team leader and/or meeting organizers. ☐

_____

_____

Meet with meeting members. ☐

_____

Figure 1.2: Pre-Meeting Steps Checklist – continued

Attend a meeting of the group. ☐

Collect information via a survey. ☐

Review information and consider potential impact on the meeting. ☐

Inside Facilitator
Review knowledge about the group and the meeting topic and consider the potential impact on the meeting. ☐

Design the Meeting

Complete:
    The Vital Agenda ☐
        Or
    The Meeting Process Design ☐

Meeting Notification ☐

Meeting Room

    Lighting ☐

    Chairs ☐

    Ease of eye contact ☐

    Temperature control ☐

    Room set-up ☐

will always clarify those objectives at the beginning of the meeting but the built-up emotions or misconceptions people bring with them can slow down the speed and effectiveness with which the group can move forward.

Inviting the wrong people has the obvious result of people wondering why they are there or a group of people with plenty of ideas but without the information or perhaps the authority to make the decisions required. An inappropriate mix of people can be just as damaging. If the climate of the group is not positive, for instance, and sensitive issues need to be discussed, it's essential that none of the participants inhibit participation inadvertently through their role or influence in the organization.

An overloaded agenda creates unrealistic expectations that cannot be met.

Even a dark cramped meeting room can have a dramatic affect on the mood and energy of the group and hence the quality of the outcomes.

The list of barriers to an effective group process that are erected by poor planning is a very long one. However some simple steps in the pre-meeting stage can eliminate each of them and give your meeting a head start to success.

There are six main points to check in this first step on the Meeting Map. Attention to the details at this stage will form the foundation of a successful meeting later.

1. Check the Meeting Objectives

Reflect on the *objective* of the meeting. **Is the wording of the objective clear?** When meeting members receive the agenda or meeting announcement, is there any room for misinterpretation of the objective? Remember that they may not have the background knowledge that you have. What makes perfect sense to you may have little meaning or a different meaning to someone with less knowledge or a different perspective.

Is the objective worthy of bringing a number of busy people together to work on it? Meetings have become a huge energy, time and economic drain on organizations. It's important to determine in advance whether a meeting is the best method to meet the objective. This is important from the point of view of efficiency but also from the perspective of the meeting process. If participants view a meeting as a waste of their time, you are going to have difficulty generating energy or thoughtful input. There are two basic reasons for bringing people together to work together toward an objective: the participants have expertise, knowledge or information that will enhance the value of the outcome and participation in the process will increase commitment to the decisions made.

Ask yourself, "Does the outcome or decision aimed for require the expertise of these individuals?" Will they actually be making the decision? If their expert input is required but the decision will ultimately be made by another group, is there another effective way to gather their input?

Is participation necessary for buy-in or is it a trivial issue that does not impact the group sufficiently for their participation to matter to them? You might want to check with the group, not just the leader on this. Sometimes what seems trivial to the leader is a hot issue for the team members or vice versa.

Is the objective realistic? Does the group have the expertise to accomplish what is required? Does the group have the authority to achieve the objective? Is the time allotted sufficient to reach the objective effectively – that is, with full participation and dialogue?

Does the size of the group allow the objectives to be met with sufficient participation in the time allotted? A rule of thumb is that if the group is larger than 10 or 12 members, in order to ensure everyone has the opportunity to participate meaningfully, the group will need to break out into smaller groups for at least some of the discussion. (We will discuss how to manage breakout groups under various topics). Using breakout groups means that more time is required: time for the small groups to relocate and get organized, discussion time (which would be required anyway), time to return to and refocus in the plenary (whole) group, and time to bring forward the points from the small group discussions and to incorporate them in a large group discussion. The final decision-making and consensus process is also likely to take longer.

2. Ensure the Right People Are Invited

Consider each member invited and check the rationale. Is each person bringing a necessary and particular expertise? Are they going to gain something from having attended? Will the implementation of the decision be made with greater ease if they are involved at the decision-making stage?

YOUR NOTES

YOUR NOTES

Too often people are invited only because the organizers are afraid of offending someone or for political purposes. In some instances this may be necessary but a more effective method of inclusion often works. Let them know about the meeting and explain the objective clearly. Let them know that you realize that this meeting might not be a good use of their time, so they are not expected to be there, but that they are welcome. Add that if they choose not to come, but wish to be updated, that will be arranged. Most people opt out but don't feel they have been overlooked.

Is there anyone missing who should be there? Are you missing any required expertise? Would it be useful to have someone who would bring an outside or devil's advocate perspective? Have members of another group had experience that they could lend to the process? If the group's objective is to make a decision, do members have the authority?

3. Learn about the Group

It is important for an outside facilitator to connect with at least some of the group members prior to the meeting. However, it can also be a good idea even if the person leading the meeting is from within the group. When working closely with others, it can be easy to assume that their take on something is the same as our own. In the fast-paced environment we are working in today, effective communication frequently does not happen.

As an outside facilitator, you need to learn as much as possible about the group and their issues, particularly those that impact the objective of the meeting you will be facilitating. The depth of information you require will depend on the nature of the meeting and the issues being addressed. If the issues are highly sensitive ones or you are leading a team building process, then ideally you will meet beforehand with each member.

The following are some questions you will need to ask in order to get the basic information required to design the meeting. If you are an inside facilitator, you will already have the answers but should reflect on them in your planning.

Questions about How the Group Works

How well do the members know one another? Have they met together before or do they meet often? If they have met together before, how successful have they been? Did they face any particular challenges?

Is this group a *work team*? If so:

- Does the team have clear goals?
- What is its level of performance on the job?
- Have there been recent success stories or challenges/difficulties?
- What is the team's climate like? Do members work well together? Can they communicate openly? Is there any conflict?
- Does the team meet regularly?
- Are its meetings effective?
- Does the team make decisions effectively?
- How does it go about making decisions?
- To what degree is the group leader-led or self-directed?
- What are the team's greatest strengths?
- What are the team's greatest opportunities for growth?
- Do team members participate fully in meetings? Are any members particularly quiet, or others dominant?

Questions about the Topic or Issue

Consider the following about the topic at hand:

- Is the topic/issue a sensitive one?
- How important is it to the group?
- What are the different perspectives on the topic of discussion?
- Are any points of view in conflict?

Gathering the Information

Any one or combination of the following methods of learning more about the group can be used:

- **A survey.** You can request that group members complete a survey anonymously and submit it directly to you, perhaps by e-mail. See Figures 1-3 through 1-6 at the end of this section for sample surveys.
  - Figure 1-3, the Team Survey, is to be used when facilitating a meeting for an internal team.
  - Figure 1-4, Information Please, is to be used if the issue to be discussed at the meeting is complex.
  - Figures 1-5 and 1-6 can be used for most groups.

- **One-on-one interviews.** This is a very important step if the issue is a sensitive one or if the theme of the session is team building. If the group is too large to interview everyone, ensure that you talk with a cross section of the members considering roles, length of time on the team or working on this project, different perspectives of the issue and authority or seniority of position.

- **Sitting in on one or more of the group's meetings.** Although people tend to be on their best behavior when outsiders attend their meeting, this is a good method of learning about how the group operates, points of view, group dynamics, as well as getting to know the individuals. An important benefit is that it gives the group a chance to get to know you. With a level of trust established, the group is likely to move ahead much more quickly in the session you lead.

4. Design the Meeting

The level of detail the meeting design requires depends on the type of meeting.

For a regular team or operational meeting, a well planned agenda is usually sufficient. For a longer and more complex meeting, often focusing on one issue such as team building or problem-solving, a more detailed design with more thought to the steps in the process is required.

Let's look at the Vital Agenda first.

Establish the Vital Agenda

The agenda is often viewed as simply a list of topics to be discussed and given little attention before the meeting. A well developed agenda, such as the Vital Agenda, as shown in Figure 1-7, can be a valuable meeting preparation and management tool.

Components of a Vital Agenda

The first column lists the **agenda items**, often the only information on a standard agenda.

The **Owner** is the person who is championing or bringing the item to the table. They are likely to be the topic expert.

For Input, Decision or Information provides meeting members with important information and clear expectations of their role in the discussion of this item.

For Information means the owner of the item will be updating the group on the item. The phrase *For Input* means members will be giving their viewpoints on the item and the information will be used by someone else to make a decision. The phrase *For Decision* means the members will be discussing the item and coming to a decision as a group.

Frequently meeting participants are frustrated that they have spent a great deal of time discussing an item and making what they thought was *the* decision only to find that the outcome was very different. This can easily happen when a group thinks they are making the decision but the owner of the item is actually only looking for input. This agenda column makes it clear who is making the decision by noting the expectation. It also indicates how much thought the member should give to the item beforehand.

- *For Input.* Sufficient thought to provide thoughtful input.
- *For Decision.* This is an important team item and deserves that members prepare accordingly.
- *For Information.* Little to no advance thinking required, unless the issue is important to the team's operation and probing questions are required.

The objective describes what is to be achieved by the end of the discussion. For example, if the item is The New Customer Service Tracking System and it is a For Information item, The Objective might be: To ensure the management team understands how to use the new system and has realistic expectations about the information it can provide.

This column then becomes a meeting management tool. At the close of the discussion, ask the group to revisit the objective and confirm that it has been met.

This column is also useful in determining which items come to the table. Is the objective substantial? If not, perhaps the information may be shared or input received another way.

The column, **Come Prepared To,** gives members specific information as to what will be expected of them in the meeting and helps ensure that meeting preparation becomes a norm for everyone. For example, "Come prepared to share two examples of difficulties you have experienced due to the new phone system" or "Come prepared to present your team's update on the spring retreat."

YOUR NOTES

Figure 1.7: The Vital Agenda

Group: ___Area A Team___

Date: ___September 25___

Meeting Leader: ___Chandra March___

Time: ___9:00 to 10:15___

Item	Owner	For Input, Decision or Information	The Objective	Come Prepared To	Allotted Time	Outcomes/ Commitments to Action
The new customer service program	Harry	For Input	To help develop an improved program	Share 2 customer service improvement ideas	30 mins.	Harry to send us an overview of the final program
Overtime hours	Sasha	For Decision	To identify methods of decreasing overtime hours	Share 1 idea for decreasing overtime hours	30 mins.	Decisions · We will deal only with level 2 customer complaints · Level 1 complaints will be passed on to Team B
Meeting Effectiveness	Chandra	Input and Decision	To improve the effectiveness of our meetings	No preparation required	15 mins.	Sue to add the two meeting improvement points to our Working Agreements and forward a copy to each member: stay on track more effectively, and ensure everyone has a chance to participate

Allotted Time indicates the time set aside for the discussion of the particular item. The completion of this column is assurance that the meeting has been thoughtfully planned.

Assigning an allotted time to each agenda item while developing the Vital Agenda ensures the meeting isn't overloaded – there is sufficient time to cover all of the items. During the meeting, you, as the facilitator, can use the allotted time column as a time management guide.

Lack of follow-through on commitments made in meetings by members is a common challenge. The **Outcomes and Commitment to Action** column brings about a dramatic change in follow-through behavior.

Ask meeting members to bring their copy of the agenda to the meeting. Have a few extra copies available in case someone forgets. If the group meets regularly, members will quickly develop the habit of bringing the Vital Agenda with them.

When an item that requires follow-up action is addressed, ask that members jot down who will do what and by when. Having team members jot down a team member's commitment emphasizes its importance and the fact that the team is depending on them.

This is also the spot to record decisions made. Completing this column ensures that each item is brought to closure effectively, with clear decisions as to the next steps. If formal meeting minutes are not required but it is important to record and communicate what was discussed and decided, the Vital Agenda can also effectively fill this need.

The Vital Agenda becomes a record of items discussed, the group's decisions and its commitments. The Commitment to Action items may become the first items on the next agenda. In this case, at the beginning of the next meeting the meeting leader asks group members to report on their progress.

The Meeting Process Design

The Meeting Process Design is a planning and organizational tool for the facilitator as well as a guide during the meeting. It provides a timetable, lists the activities (what will happen or what will be addressed), the materials you will need at each step, and process notes. Process Notes may include details of the activity including the steps or descriptions of how the actual steps will be introduced. The level of detail depends on the your

YOUR NOTES

Figure 1.8: Meeting Design Process

Group: The Gemini Team

Meeting Leader: Jason Giles

Meeting Topic: The New Client Newsletter

Objective: To review the client feedback, determine the content categories for the newsletter, and select a name for the newsletter

Time	Agenda	Materials	Process Notes
8:30	Introduction		• clarify the objective • clarify role of meeting leader • present meeting overview
8:45	Opening Energizer	15 copies of Energizer #1 from *On Track* (page 203)	1. Give an energizer example to ensure everyone understands what is expected STEP IT **Answer:** step on it or step over it 2. Conduct the energizer activity.
9:05	Develop Meeting Agreements		Aim for 6 to 8 agreements. Check for agreement on final list.
9:20	Results of Client Feedback Survey	1 copy of survey and the results for each member	Give a recap of the results. Invite questions/discussion. Ask members to identify content categories suggested by the survey results.
9:50	Identify Newsletter Content Categories	Copy of Decision-Making Criteria Grid for each member (*On Track*, page 215)	Break large group into 4 smaller groups. Assign a discussion leader to each group. Ask groups to return to the larger group in 50 minutes with their recommendations for 5 content categories and having taken a 10 minute break. Bring groups back together. Discuss recommendations. Look for commonalities. If consensus on the content categories does not evolve from the discussion, use the Decision-Making Criteria Grid.

Figure 1.8: Meeting Design Process – continued

Time	Agenda	Materials	Process Notes
11:50	Process Check.		Ask: "What can we do differently this afternoon to work together even more effectively?"
12:00	Lunch		
1:00	After lunch energizer	15 copies of Energizer #4 from *On Track* (page 209)	Conduct the game.
1.10	Brainstorm Newsletter Names	Slide of Brainstorming Steps (*On Track*, page 124)	Review brainstorming steps and rules. Divide larger group into 4 new groups. Ask small groups to use the brainstorming technique and return in 30 mins with an idea for a Newsletter name. Share and discuss the ideas.
2:10	Creativity Check		Ask "Could we put a more creative twist on any of the names we have come up with?"
2:25	Select the Name	sticky dots	Review the names suggested. If there is not immediate agreement, use multi-voting.
3:00	Recap and Commitment to Action		Decide on next steps. Congratulate the group on their accomplishment.

familiarity and comfort level with the steps – less comfort or less experience will mean more detailed notes. Process notes are reminders that meeting facilitators write to themselves. Figure 1-8 provides an example of a completed Meeting Process Design.

If you are new to the meeting facilitator role, return to this after you have examined the tools and techniques presented in Chapters 3 through 7.

Caution	Beware of Being Overly Attached to the Design

 Lack of structure is dangerous, but so is an inflexible structure or design. You may spend hours designing a meeting process and then find that the group objectives will be best met by deviating from it.

This does not mean that the original design was not a good one. When a group of people come together effectively, new ideas and directions may emerge. Better plans may evolve from the original structure, but its development provides the critical foundation.

5. Meeting Notification

When meetings don't work, they often start going downhill even before people get into the room. When people don't understand what the meeting is about and therefore don't understand its importance, it's hard to make a meeting a priority. Participants may become no-shows or appear with a "why am I wasting my time here?" mindset.

Equally important, if people don't understand the purpose of the meeting, they cannot come prepared. Communication before the meeting is as important as communication within the meeting.

If you are an outside facilitator, ask the leader to introduce you in the meeting notification and follow up with a brief note from yourself telling the group you are looking forward to working with them. You might also ask them to provide you with certain information, perhaps via a brief survey or give them a brief assignment in preparation for the meeting.

6. Choose and Organize the Best Meeting Space

The physical environment can have a dramatic impact on the success of your meeting. Although there is the occasional situation in which you have to "make do," make every effort to ensure the best possible meeting space.

When choosing a meeting space, check the features below.

Lighting

Often the last factor to be considered, lighting, particularly for a meeting of several hours duration, is one of the most important aspects of the meeting environment. It affects not only the participants' basic ability to read any documents provided, but it also strongly influences mood and energy levels.

Look for soft (not dim) natural lighting. The best possible scenario is a room with plenty of windows, equipped with window coverings to handle the glare from the sun.

Chairs

Try out the chairs. Look for well-padded chairs with back support. If they are adjustable, all the better.

Ease of Eye Contact

Ensure there are no obstacles such as pillars that will prevent participants from seeing you and *vice versa*, or from seeing one another.

Temperature Control

Meeting members tend to be like hot house flowers – to flower they need just the right temperature. Both cold and heat distract them. Ideally choose a room in which you can personally control the temperature. If this is not possible, check that it can be quickly controlled with a phone call (get the number and keep it handy). If you are not sure of the reliability of the temperature control, suggest that participants come dressed in layers.

Room Set-up

Your aim is to create an environment for dialogue. Once again, eye contact is important. If the group is large (over 12 people), round tables, accommodating six to eight people each, work best to encourage dialogue. Everyone can see and hear one another easily. Tables should be far enough apart so that the discussion of one group will not interfere with another.

Smaller groups can work well around a board room table, tables arranged in a U-shape, or in an informal setting of sofas and easy chairs.

YOUR NOTES

Figure 1.3: Team Survey

To _____   Re _____

From _____   Date of Meeting _____

Please respond to the following questions. The information will help me prepare for our meeting.

I do not require your names.

Thanks for your assistance.

Please rate each of the following statements on a scale of 1 to 4. 1—this never describes our meetings; 2—occasionally; 3—usually; 4—always/definitely. Feel free to add comments.

The team has clear goals   1   2   3   4
If rating a 3 or 4, list two goals.

_____

We are a high performance team.   1   2   3   4
If rating a 3 or 4, describe two recent achievements.

_____

Members work well together.   1   2   3   4
Provide an example to support your rating.

_____

Members pull in the same direction.   1   2   3   4
Provide an example to support your rating.

_____

We feel supported by the organization.   1   2   3   4
Provide an example to support your rating.

_____

We are kept well informed.   1   2   3   4
Provide an example to support your rating.

_____

We share information readily with one another.   1   2   3   4
Provide an example to support your rating.

_____

We share knowledge readily with one another.   1   2   3   4
Provide an example to support your rating.

_____

Team members take initiative.   1   2   3   4
Provide an example to support your rating.

_____

Figure 1.4: Information Please

To _____   Re _____

From _____   Date of Meeting _____

The objective of our meeting is _____
_____

Please answer the following questions to assist me in preparing for the meeting.

Thanks for your help.

_____

List the key issues that relate to our objective.

_____
_____
_____

Briefly describe the different perspectives that members hold on key points. Please put an * beside your own perspective.

_____
_____
_____

If you believe we will face any challenges in meeting our objective, please describe them briefly.

_____
_____
_____

If you have identified challenges, how do you believe we can best overcome them?

_____
_____
_____

Figure 1.5: Meeting Style Survey

To _____   Re _____

From _____   Date of Meeting _____

Please respond to the following questions. The information will help me prepare for our meeting.

I do not require your names.

Thanks for your assistance.

Please rate each of the following statements on a scale of 1 to 4. 1—this never describes our meetings; 2—occasionally; 3—usually; 4—always/definitely. Feel free to add comments.

	1	2	3	4
People arrive on time.	1	2	3	4
We have full participation.	1	2	3	4
We have no discussion monopolizers.	1	2	3	4
We have open and honest communication.	1	2	3	4
People are open to new ideas.	1	2	3	4
Discussions stay on track.	1	2	3	4
We manage our time well.	1	2	3	4
We challenge each other's thinking.	1	2	3	4
We introduce creative ideas/solutions.	1	2	3	4
We use effective problem solving and decision making methods.	1	2	3	4
We achieve consensus with ease.	1	2	3	4
Decisions are fully supported by group members.	1	2	3	4
We follow through on commitments made.	1	2	3	4

Other comments _____

_____

_____

Figure 1.6: Work Environment Survey

Usually completed in an interview with team leader(s) or meeting organizers. May be completed by meeting members.

1. How would you rate the climate within the organization?

1	2	3	4
low			high

    _____

    _____

2. Describe any recent events that may be affecting the climate.

    _____

    _____

3. Does your organization have a history of following through on action items that come out of meetings?

1	2	3	4
no			definitely/always

    _____

    _____

4. Describe any recent decisions/changes that have a significant impact on this group who will be meeting.

    _____

    _____

5. Describe any significant organizational changes not listed in 2 or 4.

    _____

    _____

THE OPENING

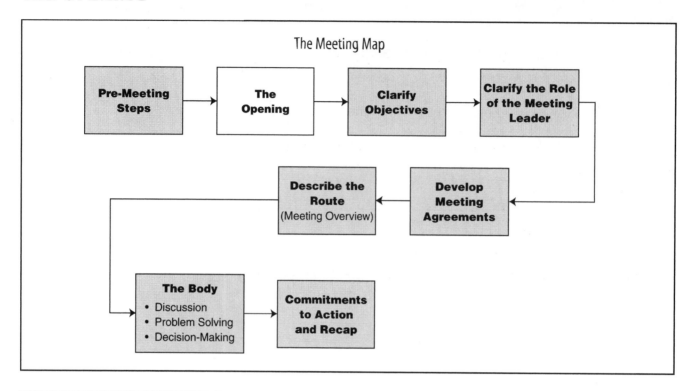

The Meeting Map

YOUR NOTES

This step is a very short, but important leg of the meeting journey. What you say and do in the first few minutes can have a powerful impact on the ease and effectiveness with which the rest of the meeting unfolds. These first few words can set the tone, increase the comfort level, increase commitment to the group process that lies ahead, and move people mentally into the meeting. For those who aren't seasoned meeting leaders, getting started on the right foot is also a great confidence booster allowing you to move ahead smoothly.

What you refer to in the first few minutes is not important. What is important is that you have thought about it beforehand and that you deliver the words with attention-getting energy.

Don't move too quickly into information that it is important for everyone hear. Approximately 25% of meeting members are not mentally with you for the first few minutes. They may be thinking about the work they left on their desk, checking out who is in the room, or if they don't know you, they may be sizing you up.

Meeting Energizers

A brief energizing activity can be a good way to start a meeting. Good energizers, such as brainteasers, assist you in several ways: they ensure people are mentally with you, they get people communicating and working together and they also encourage more creative thinking. I have found that starting the meeting with an exercise that forces people to use a thinking pattern that is usually different from their day-to-day thinking style increases the likelihood that creative or breakthrough thinking will happen during the meeting.

For a few samples of brainteaser activities you might turn to the Worksheets section at the back of this book.

Some facilitators are hesitant to use activities like this for fear that the no nonsense, busy group they are about to lead would think it a waste of time. I have yet to bump into a group that didn't enjoy and see the benefit of beginning a meeting this way. However, if you are hesitant, explain upfront why you are asking them to participate in the activity by sharing the benefits described above. Emphasize that it will only take a few minutes.

YOUR NOTES

CLARIFY OBJECTIVES

The Meeting Map

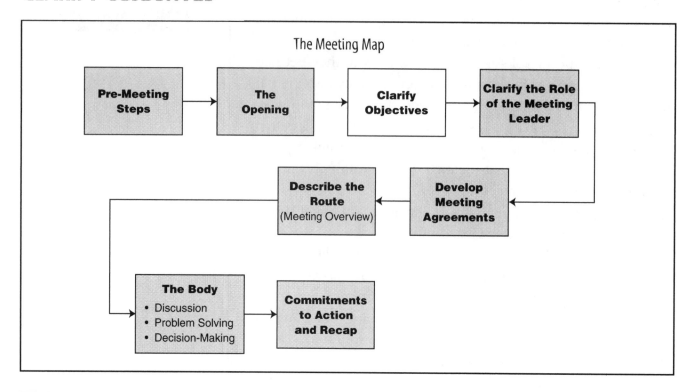

YOUR NOTES

No matter how apparently obvious the objective, as meeting leader, you should never assume it is understood, or understood in the same way, by all the members.

Clearly understood objectives are essential to:

- The meeting discussion remaining focused and on track.
- Preventing miscommunication and even negative conflict.
- Quality decisions.

Whether or not you spend five minutes to clarify objectives at the beginning of the meeting can determine the success of the meeting.

How to Describe and Use Objectives

Meeting leaders often assume that meeting members know why they are there. There may be reasons to reasonably assume this. If you planned well, members will have received a meeting notification, which stated the purpose of the meeting or an agenda that outlined agenda topics. On the other hand, it is not unusual for meeting invitees to receive nothing other than a call to a meeting. But even having been given some information as to purpose doesn't mean people know why they are there. People are inundated by information and often don't do a good job of selecting what they need and don't need. They may have paid attention to the bare bones, time and place, may have briefly skimmed the meeting objective, misunderstood it or forgotten it.

If you use the Vital Agenda described earlier, people should come with a better understanding of the objective. However, never assume understanding. Clarifying the objective takes only a few minutes and provides critical focus.

The objective describes what the group wants to achieve. For example: To decide upon a new customer fulfillment strategy for the warehouse and to confirm next steps, when they will be taken and by whom.

The prime objective is to decide upon the new strategy but it is useful to include the required follow-through steps that must be agreed upon. That is, in this case confirm the next steps, when they will be taken and by whom.

This confirms to the group that there will be closure and follow-through and therefore the meeting will be worthwhile. It lets people know what to expect so that they are not picking up their things, ready to leave as soon as the decision is made. It allows for appropriate timing, reminding the group that the closure items will require some time. It reminds the meeting leader to manage the time accordingly.

Other examples of clear objectives could read as follows:

- To develop a recommendation for management as to how to most effectively restructure the shipping department and to decide who will present the recommendations, when and how those individuals will report back to the group.
- To provide the marketing department with input on the new product advertising copy, specifically whether the copy reflects the key features and benefits of the product design.

In the last example, it is clear that the group is not only there to provide input but specific input on whether the features and benefits have been described.

The most common complaint about meetings is that they too often stray off topic. When this happens it is frequently because the objective is not understood in the same way by everyone or has been forgotten.

YOUR NOTES

YOUR NOTES

When the objective is specific and the group is reminded of the objective as needed, discussions stay focused.

Caution	Set Objectives Before the Meeting

Meeting leaders, intending to be facilitative, sometimes ask for agreement with the objective or invite people to add to or change it. On rare occasions, this is appropriate but most often this practise is risky. When you invite people for different ideas, someone will inevitably come up with one. The entire meeting can be derailed and the time set aside to meet the objective used in re-establishing the objective.

If you sense that the objective may not take the group where they need to go, deal with it in your pre-meeting planning. However, if during the meeting it appears that the objective may not be appropriate, definitely stop and check whether the objective is valid.

The Objective as a Meeting Management Tool

When you describe the objective at the outset of the meeting, also remind the group about the time allotted for the meeting.

Ideally the objective is posted or on a slide that can easily be put up. It is a very useful tool for the facilitator to use during the discussion and should be kept handy. If at any point, the discussion strays, refer to the objective and ask the group, "Is this discussion moving us toward our objective?"

The group may be discussing something it sees as important, but which is not directly related to the objective. If the group has the authority to decide what is accomplished during the meeting, point out to them the time left and ask whether they wish to continue the present discussion and leave the meeting's objective until next meeting; whether they wish to park the present discussion until a later date for future discussion; or whether the group is now happy to set it aside permanently and move on to the objective at hand. Check carefully for consensus on this. A small vocal group may feel this "hot" topic is more important than the original objective, but many others may feel their time is being wasted if the original objective is not met.

If the group's objective has been prescribed and what is covered in the meeting is not their choice to make, use the Parking Lot tip.

Try This   The Parking Lot

The Parking Lot is a classic technique for dealing with "stray discussion." Title a flip chart page or laptop screen "Parking Lot." When the group or a member begins talking about an issue that is not directly related to the objective of the meeting, "park" it on the flipchart. This confirms to the individuals that they have been heard. The group must decide whether and how to carry parked ideas forward, so they are not lost.

YOUR NOTES

CLARIFY THE ROLE OF THE MEETING LEADER

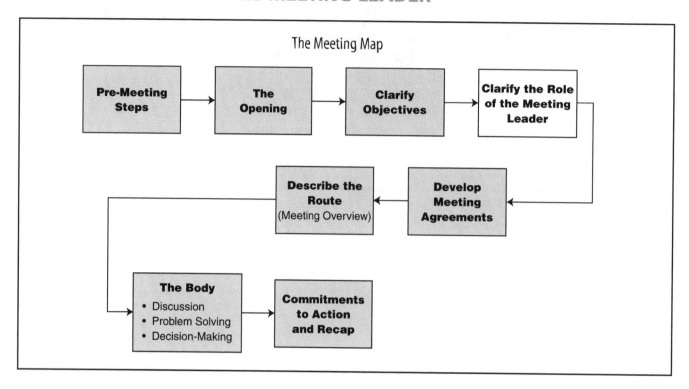

The Meeting Map

YOUR NOTES

Clarifying your role as the meeting facilitator ensures meeting members have realistic expectations and gives you permission to take action or intervene as needed to ensure a successful meeting.

Expectations might include:

- If you are the team leader or manager of the group that is meeting, members might expect you to lead the discussion but then make the final decision.
- If you are an outside facilitator, the group might expect you to act also as a content expert or consultant.

These may or may not be accurate and realistic expectations. Describing your role will ensure that the group's expectations of you are realistic and that all members have the same understanding of your role.

Describing your role also prepares members for actions you might take and so increases your own comfort in using them. For example, you might say, "My responsibility as facilitator is to ensure that we work together effectively so that the objectives we have described are met. In order to do that, there may be times when I may play devil's advocate, invite someone to par-

YOUR NOTES

ticipate or ask someone to shorten their comments in order to accomplish what is needed within the allotted time."

What you choose to describe as your responsibility will depend on the group and the issues at hand, i.e., the behaviors that you anticipate may require management.

Explaining your role can be particularly useful if for any reason you feel hesitant to intercede. Perhaps, for example, the CEO is in the meeting and you anticipate his taking over the meeting. You have declared upfront that you will interrupt people if the need should arise. In doing this, you have given yourself permission, the group has been reminded and the task becomes much easier.

Try This | Facilitator Versus Team Member

 As an inside meeting facilitator, whether the team leader or a member, use a discussion with the team to clarify your role. Include points such as what do we expect from a team member who leads our meetings, how can they balance the need to be an objective meeting facilitator with the need to share their ideas and knowledge as a team member.

DEVELOP MEETING AGREEMENTS

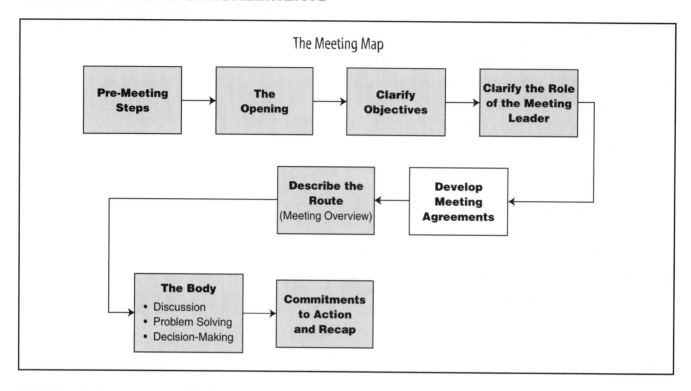

The Meeting Map

```
Pre-Meeting     →     The          →     Clarify      →     Clarify the Role
Steps                 Opening            Objectives         of the Meeting
                                                            Leader
                                                                  │
                                                                  ↓
Describe the    ←     Develop
Route                 Meeting
(Meeting Overview)    Agreements
      │
      ↓
The Body        →     Commitments
• Discussion          to Action
• Problem Solving     and Recap
• Decision-Making
```

YOUR NOTES

At this step, you, as the meeting leader, invite meeting members to identify behaviors that must be consistently demonstrated by members if they are to meet their meeting objectives. The behaviors identified and agreed to become the Meeting Agreements for the meeting or, in the case of a group that meets regularly, they may be used on an ongoing basis.

A Working Agreement might go something like this: "We agree consensus means we will each support the decisions made after we leave the meeting" or "We agree to check our understanding of a member's comment before disapproving or adding our own."

The set of Meeting Agreements is your power tool. In developing them, the group recognizes that the behaviors described are important and expects you, the meeting leader, to ensure that the group members demonstrate them. In effect, the group is empowering you to manage these behaviors.

Meeting Agreements: The Meeting Leader's Power Tool

Meeting Agreements describe positive behaviors the group has identified as very important to working together effectively. Meeting Agreements are often referred to as ground rules or norms. However, people tend to be more receptive to the idea of agreements than rules. The term norms is not always fully understood by meeting members. The term Meeting Agreements is easily understood and suggests the group is involved in their development, rather than subject to a set of rules being imposed. (See Figure 1-9 for a sample set of meeting agreements.)

Meeting agreements are your power tool. Use them well. Before we look at how to develop them, let's reflect for a moment where you are on the Meeting Map (Figure 1-1).

You have clarified the objective, described your role in the process and given an overview of the steps the group will take in the meeting to achieve the objectives. At this point, you will invite the group to develop Meeting Agreements. In doing so you are asking them to think about how they need to work together to achieve their objectives in the time allotted.

You might say, "We have established our objectives and we each want to leave this meeting feeling that it has been a productive and positive experience. What do you believe is important for each of us to keep in mind in order to ensure this happens?" or "I need your help in ensuring that this meeting is a highly productive one and rewarding for everyone. What behaviors do you believe we must demonstrate if we are to have a successful meeting?"

Try This	Take the Backdoor to Meeting Agreements

 If you feel the group may not be receptive to the idea of developing meeting agreements (perhaps they are in a hurry, have developed ground rules before that haven't worked), don't introduce the idea of Meeting Agreements. You might use the sample questions described in the text. Collect the ideas and then check for agreement. At this stage you might jot the heading Meeting Agreements at the top of the list.

Getting Everyone into It

You can ensure everyone is involved in developing the agreements by using the following steps:

1. Pose the question as described above.
2. Invite group members to think to themselves and jot down their ideas on their notepad.

Figure 1.9: Sample Meeting Agreements

We agree:

- To participate fully.

- To keep our comments on track.

- To listen to all ideas.

- To keep our discussion confidential.

- To focus on how things work, rather than why they won't work.

- To ensure no one dominates the discussion.

- To fully support all decisions made.

3. If there are 10 or fewer members, go around the group round robin fashion and record the ideas on a flip chart or board under the heading Meeting Agreements. If the group is larger, invite members to "throw out" their ideas.

4. Briefly discuss the ideas. Most agreements describe common sense behaviors that people just forget to demonstrate and in-depth discussion is seldom needed.

5. Confirm consensus on the group's set of working agreements.

6. Post the agreements where they are visible and can be easily referred to during the meeting.

If there are more than 10 group members, everyone may not have verbally contributed ideas but the silent generation of ideas in step two ensures that they are participating in that they have given the question some thought.

Members' responses are usually based on previous negative experiences. For example, if they frequently attend meetings that are not on track they may say, "We must make sure that our comments are focused on the task at hand." If they have experienced situations in which some people have monopolized the meeting you will hear, "We have to make sure that everyone has the opportunity to participate."

There is no right or wrong list. Your agreements will vary depending on the experience of the group. If you feel important agreements or behaviors have been missed, feel free to add them. Important agreements address any negative behavior that you think likely to arise in the group.

Your ability to identify any gaps in the agreement list will depend on how well you know the group, either through previous experience with them or from your pre-meeting information gathering. You might say, "There is another agreement that I would like to recommend we adopt. ... Can everyone agree to it?"

Aim for seven or eight agreements. It is a short enough list to be manageable, but long enough to cover key behaviors.

Check for consensus on the final set of agreements. This is essential to ensure that each member owns all of the agreements, not only the ones they contributed.

YOUR NOTES

YOUR NOTES

Try This   Make It Specific!

Agreements work best when they describe very specific behavior. For example, consider, "Everyone must respect one another." Members may have different perceptions as to what respect looks like behaviorally. If a suggestion arises that doesn't describe a specific behavior, ask the group to be more specific. For example you may ask, "What will tell you that members are respecting one another?" You are likely to get responses such as, "People will listen to one another." "People will not shoot down each others' ideas." In the agreements, capture the specific behaviors described.

Using the Agreements

If the agreements aren't referred to, their development will be seen as a time-wasting exercise.

How often you refer to them depends on the length of the meeting and the type of behavior demonstrated by the members. If you observe behavior that does not reflect that which has been agreed to, ask the members to pause their discussion for a few minutes and invite them to reflect on their process. You might say, "Let's stop our discussion for just a moment and remind ourselves of our Meeting Agreements." Briefly review the list and then ask, "How are we doing?" You might also invite participants to identify any agreements that aren't being lived up to. If no one responds, describe what you have observed.

Bring the group's attention back to the agreements at least once during the meeting and ask simply, "How well are we living up to our agreements?" This reminds the group of the behaviors they have agreed to demonstrate and of the importance of the group process. If members have demonstrated nonproductive behaviors that were not addressed in the original Meeting Agreements, you can ask if now that the group has spent some time working together, they would like to add any agreements. If group members have not noticed the non-productive behavior or are hesitant to address it, share your observation.

Caution	Beware Undeveloped Agreements

Meeting Agreements that aren't well developed and well used can be dangerous.

Well developed agreements result from full participation; describe specific behaviors; are fully agreed to.

Well used agreements are reviewed on a regular basis and used to challenge the group to enhance its group process.

When the Group is Ongoing

If the group is ongoing and meets regularly, review the agreements briefly before each meeting. As the group develops over time, its Meeting Agreements should reflect that growth. Agreements that are always lived up to and have become norms can be removed from the list. It is likely however that new agreements will be required. For example at the "getting to know you" stage, full participation is often one of the Agreements. Once everyone is comfortable there may be full participation, but members may be so open that they are not sensitive to how others may receive their comments.

In this instance, an agreement such as "We agree to participate fully" might be removed. However, "We agree to be sensitive in giving feedback" may be added.

The Benefits

Effectively developing and using Meeting Agreements reminds members that each person is responsible for the success of the meeting. It creates a sense of shared responsibility for the success of the meeting. Establishing Meeting Agreements also ensures that all members have thought about the *process* and the behaviors that create a positive and productive group process. As well, participants are alerted to behaviors that hinder the process, before turning their attention to the *task* or *content* of the meeting.

Meeting Agreements also empower the facilitator by giving you "permission" to lead the group according to the agreements. This permission may be especially important when you perform the roles of the group leader and also a team member. Meeting Agreements encourage team members to adjust any personal behavior that may negatively affect the group process.

YOUR NOTES

In the case of ongoing teams, agreements become not just a group process management tool, but a growth management tool. The question will become, "What do we need to do differently to become even more effective than we already are?" Each agreement that is removed, marks team growth in the behavior described in that agreement. New agreements describe new growth opportunities.

Caution	Beware Limp Agreements

Limp agreements are those that are ineffective or which hinder the group process. Examples include:

- *A standard set of agreements passed around the organization from meeting to meeting. One size does **not** fit all when it comes to meeting agreements.*
- *A set of agreements written by the meeting leader and presented to the group as a finished product.*
- *Agreements that once written are forgotten.*
- *Agreements that don't describe specific behaviors.*
- *Agreements that don't have consensus.*

DESCRIBE THE ROUTE

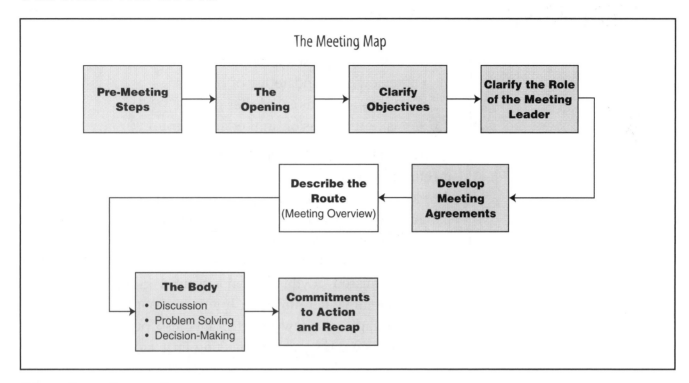

Meeting Overview

By this spot on the map, you will have the group's attention, they will understand their objective and the time in which they must complete it, and will have developed Meeting Agreements.

Some meeting members, particularly those who work best within a structured environment, will focus more effectively on the task at hand if you give them a preview of the steps they will be going through to meet the objective. Those steps will vary greatly depending on the meeting. Here is an example.

"Kathleen has joined us to provide some additional information on the project and we will have an opportunity to ask her questions. Once we have all of the information we need to make a decision, we will review the list of options identified at our last meeting and we will check whether the new information suggests any additional options. Once we have confirmed the list of options, I suggest we break into smaller groups to ensure that everyone has a chance to fully participate. Each group will be asked to come back to the larger group with a first and second choice of options and their rationale for each. We will compare notes, look for commonalities and come to consensus on the preferred option. I will provide you with the timing and specific instructions for each step as we go along."

YOUR NOTES

YOUR NOTES

To ensure this is clear and succinct, put three or four bullet points on a slide or flipchart. For example, you might list the following:

- Kathleen's presentation.
- Review and update list of options.
- Discuss options in smaller groups.
- Make the decision in the larger group.

Although presenting the overview is an early step in the meeting process, you won't be able to draft it until you have developed the whole meeting process. At this point in your planning, make a note to yourself to return to this step.

Writing this overview is also a very helpful exercise for you. You will be able to check whether it "feels" right and whether you have missed anything. Condensing a group process that could range anywhere from an hour to a couple of days into a brief paragraph or a few bullet points also puts it into a manageable package for you, the meeting facilitator.

THE BODY

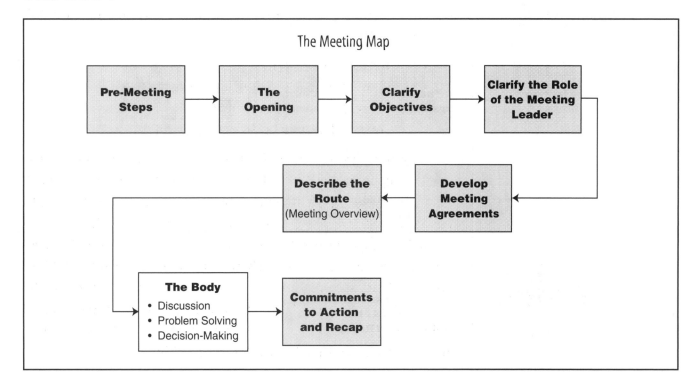

The Meeting Map

Pre-Meeting Steps → The Opening → Clarify Objectives → Clarify the Role of the Meeting Leader

Describe the Route (Meeting Overview) ← Develop Meeting Agreements

The Body
• Discussion
• Problem Solving
• Decision-Making

Commitments to Action and Recap

This spot on the Meeting Map is where the bulk of the work that the group has been assigned gets done. You will spend most of your meeting time at this point. The task will be accomplished through discussion, problem solving and decision-making. The tools and techniques you will require to lead the group through each of these processes are provided in the chapters that follow.

Caution	Highly Task-Oriented Group

Although the Body of the meeting is where you will spend most of your time getting the job done, the previous steps are essential to your success here. A highly task-oriented group might send messages that they want to skip the introductory steps and jump right into the discussion. If you are certain that you are working with a highly seasoned group, you might move through the initial steps more quickly but never eliminate them completely. Remember, you are the person who has been appointed the process expert, the group members are the content experts.

YOUR NOTES

COMMITMENTS TO ACTION AND RECAP

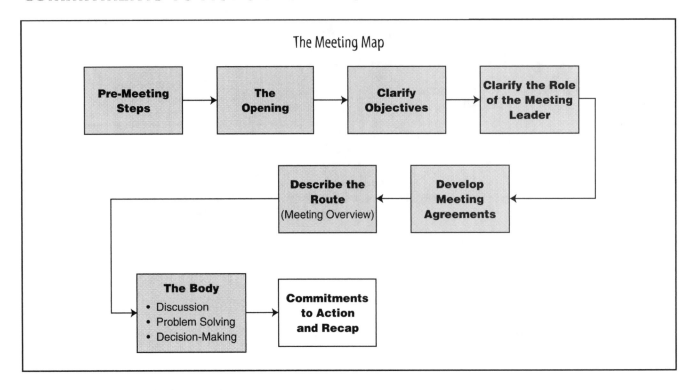

The Meeting Map

YOUR NOTES

The importance of not jumping too quickly into the task has been discussed but it is just as important that you don't wind up too quickly. Too often, groups run out of time and people are dashing out the door to the next meeting or to pick up the kids before the discussion has been properly brought to closure.

Time your discussion to leave sufficient time for commitment to action and a recap, the last stop on the Meeting Map. The length of time required depends on the number and complexity of the outcomes or decisions but a general rule of thumb is at least 10 minutes.

In this step, the group should return to each decision or outcome and ensure that the next steps have been captured, including *who* will do *what* and *when*. If you are using the Vital Agenda (Figure 1-7), suggest meeting members jot these next steps down in the last column. Then do a quick recap of everything decided. You might say "Let me do a quick recap before we leave to ensure we all have the same understanding of what we have agreed to."

Benefits

Reviewing the commitments to action and recapping the decisions has the following benefits:

- Prevents the post-meeting "I didn't think *that* was what we decided" syndrome.
- Confirms consensus.
- Increases the likelihood that individuals will follow through on commitments made in the meeting.
- Ensures that meeting members leave the meeting with a sense of accomplishment.

YOUR NOTES

Each step of the map is extremely important when leading a focused group process in which the group must discuss an issue in-depth, make important decisions and come to agreement on them.

The Benefit of Using the Meeting Map

- The Map helps provide the structure that is often missing from meetings that don't work well.
- The Map acts as a guide for the facilitator and helps boost the confidence of new facilitators.
- The Map ensures no steps essential to meeting success are overlooked.

All of the steps described in the Map earlier in this chapter are relevant to regular, ongoing meetings. You will, however, use some of the steps differently and may change the order. See Figure 1-9 to view what your meeting map could look like.

Pre-Meeting Steps

How much pre-meeting work is required will depend, for the most part, on the nature of the agenda items, however, two key steps are:

- Developing a Vital Agenda (Figure 1-7).
- Ensuring the right people are involved (page 17).

The Opening

Plan your opening statement and deliver it confidently to ensure the meeting starts decisively and energetically, rather than, "Well, is everyone ready to start?" Consider using the Meeting Energizers in the Worksheets section at the back of this book.

Clarify the Role of the Meeting Leader

This is extremely important but is usually a one time happening for regular meetings led by a team member or the team leader. It is important to make a group decision on the expectations of the meeting leader and how the challenges of the dual role of meeting facilitator and meeting participant or stakeholder will be met (see How Can a Leader Best Facilitate Meetings When They Are A Team Member? in Chapter 11, page 161). Once the expectations of the role have been defined, revisit it at meetings occasionally to check members are fulfilling the role as defined and/or whether the definition of the role needs to be changed.

Develop Meeting Agreements

The development of a set of Meeting Agreements is a one time event. However, agreements should be reviewed before each meeting and updated from time to time.

Describe the Route: Meeting Overview

Provide a quick preview of items to be discussed, an introduction of any guests, and their role in the meeting and the meeting timeframe.

Clarify Objectives

An objective will be tied to each item brought to the meeting. Ensure members understand what is meant to be achieved by discussing the item.

The Body

As described earlier in this chapter, the body of the meeting is the stage where you will spend the most time. It is here that you deal with the items brought to the meeting. The bulk of the discussion, the problem-solving and the decision-making will occur at this step.

Commitment to Action and Meeting Recap

Provide a recap of decisions, outcomes and commitments to action.

Check your meeting effectiveness. If your meetings need considerable improvement, do this at the end of each meeting. Otherwise do a meeting effectiveness check periodically.

When using the Map for regular meetings, you will repeat the following three steps for each agenda item:

1. Clarify the objectives.
2. The Body of the meeting (discussion, problem-solving or decision-making).
3. Commitments to action.

YOUR NOTES

Chapter 2

Making Powerful Decisions

ere we come to the nub of the matter. Ultimately the quality of the decisions made is what reflects the effectiveness with which the group has worked. If you've planned the meeting carefully, using the Vital Agenda, you've maximized your chances of success. All of the tools and steps provided in *On Track* are designed to help you facilitate groups in such a way that they will go far beyond mediocrity in meeting their objectives. Their decisions will make a difference.

The quality of a decision reflects the quality of the process that produced it.

ENCOUNTERING A DECISION-MAKING POTHOLE

There are several factors that together result in effective decision making. Their absence can create what I think of as potholes in the decision-making process. At the very least, the potholes are rough on the group that has to get over them; if the potholes are deep enough, the decision-making process can be severely damaged or even stuck.

It is evident when a group has hit a decision-making pothole. The more aware you are of the symptoms, the greater the likelihood that you will be able to see them ahead and facilitate the group around them.

Symptoms of Decision-Making Potholes

The following list offers some of the symptoms that your group has hit or is approaching a decision-making pothole:

- Wheel spinning.
- Off-track or off-topic discussions.
- Moving too slowly toward a decision.
- Jumping too quickly to a decision.
- Rigid points of view.
- Conflict.
- Members who have tuned out.
- Members who say little but whose body language suggests that they have a strong opinion.
- Members who reluctantly agree, giving in to the group or an individual or giving up on an ineffective process.
- Mediocre solutions.
- Lack of energy or enthusiasm.
- Few ideas.
- Resorting to majority rule because the group can't achieve consensus.

Decision-making potholes are created when the following factors are absent:

- An objective that is understood and agreed to.
- A structured process.
- The right decision-making method for the scenario.
- An understanding of who is making the final decision.
- Using the best decision-making tools.
- Sufficient information and knowledge.
- The right members at the table.
- Sufficient and well-managed time.
- Positive group behaviors.
- Innovative thinking.
- Reflection time.

When these factors are present, your result is *powerful decisions that are energetically supported by the group members.* Your meeting success is not only measured immediately by people leaving the meeting room with the *that was a great meeting* feeling, but also when the highly effective decisions are implemented.

Finding The Right Way

When members aren't happy with a decision, it is frequently not the decision itself that creates the discomfort but the *way* the decision was made.

When a group produces inferior decisions, it is usually not because of lack of knowledge or ability but because of the *way* the decisions were made.

The *way* can include all aspects of an effective meeting process. But more specifically, the way to excellent decisions includes selecting and agreeing to the best decision-making method and using decision-making tools effectively.

IMPORTANT – Before jumping into making decisions, take time to describe and get agreement from the group on the decision-making method.

Caution	It's Not the Decision

When members do not fully support a decision, it is often not because they are unhappy with the decision itself. It is frequently the way the decision was made that makes them unhappy.

DECISION-MAKING METHODS

You have three decision-making options:

- One person or another makes the decision.
- The decision is made through consensus of the group.
- A majority vote of the group members determines the decision.

Option 1: One Person or Another Group

In this method, the decision is made by one person or another group. This is obviously not a group decision-making process but poor understanding of this option or poor use often impedes the group process. Within this method are two possible scenarios.

It could be that the decision is one that the team does not have the power to make or influence. It is being made by the leader, perhaps senior management or a group somewhere else in the organization. The topic is being brought to the meeting to inform group members. The meeting process goes off track when the group becomes involved in a non-productive discussion about something they cannot influence.

Alternatively, an item is brought to the group for their input but someone else is making the decision. Problems arise here when the group is simply asked "What do you think about ...?" and who is making the decision or how the group's input will be used is not made clear. When this hasn't been explained in advance, groups are often frustrated when the final decision does not reflect their input. They feel that they haven't been listened to or the process was a waste of time because they didn't understand that their role in the decision-making process was limited to giving input, which may or may not sway the decision.

Another scenario could have the group empower one individual to make a particular decision. This is an important option that is underused. Groups frequently indulge in over participation, that is they make too many group decisions that could effectively be made by one person. When should the group pass the decision to one person or smaller group? Consider passing the decision on:

- If one person or a smaller group is accountable for the outcome.
- If it is a decision that does not have a major impact on the group's results.
- If members do not have strong opinions on the topic.
- If one person or a small group are the experts on the subject.
- Ultimately, if having the entire group make the decision adds no value.

Option 2: Consensus

Most groups see consensus as the ideal method. At the same time, many groups find it the most difficult to achieve. The greatest impediments to consensus are misunderstanding or different understandings of what consensus means.

Definitions range from "a decision with which there is wholehearted, 100% agreement" to "a decision everyone can live with."

The first can sometimes be achieved, but is often an unrealistic expectation; the second does not aim high enough. "Living with it" doesn't suggest the energy or enthusiasm that will be required to make the decision work. The definition of consensus that most effectively guides consensus reaching processes is – *willingness to support the decision 100%.*

Steps to Achieving Consensus

1. **Confirm that consensus is required.** Consensus is required when one or more of the following apply:

- The group is addressing an important issue.
- The group members are directly affected by the decision.
- The members' understanding and behavior can affect whether the decision works. Buy-in is required.

2. **Post the definition of consensus.** Consensus is willingness to support the decision 100%. Discuss the definition. Invite members to describe their understanding of the word "support." Ensure that it is agreed that *support* includes:

- Speaking positively about the decision and taking ownership for the decision outside of the meeting, i.e. "We decided – not they decided."
- Doing whatever is required to make the decision work.

Members' support will depend more on how they see the process, than on whether they like the decision. In order for a member to fully support a decision, they must know that their ideas and concerns have been heard and must understand (not necessarily agree with) the rationale for the decision. The majority of people, when championing an idea, don't take sufficient time to explain their thinking. Ensuring that people feel heard and understood is a priority for meeting leaders.

Caution   100% Support

Occasionally group members quibble about 100% support. It should not be an issue. If members agree to support the decision there should not be degrees of support. However, if you believe the group could get bogged down in a discussion of 100% and what that means, remove it from the definition. That is, consensus means willingness to support the decision. Ensure the group agrees to the meaning of **support**.

YOUR NOTES

YOUR NOTES

Handle with Care   Closed Minds Hamper the Process

True consensus, particularly when the issue is sensitive, can occur only when members listen openly to one another. The structured processes suggested throughout this book support that happening.

3. **Agree on a back-up plan.** Should the group not be able to achieve consensus, how will the decision be made (this does not happen often if tools are used well, unless the group is highly dysfunctional or the decision particularly sensitive)? Back-up plans could include:

- Passing the decision to the leader or the person most directly involved in making the decision work.
- Deciding by majority vote.
- If all members agree to *support* whatever decision is made via a back-up plan, in essence you have achieved consensus.

4. **Use tools that effectively structure the process.** See Tools of the Trade (Chapter 3), including:

- The Generating and Organizing Ideas Technique
- Force Field Analysis
- Pros and Cons Chart
- Multi-Voting
- Priority Sequencing
- The Decision-Making Criteria Grid.

5. **Confirm Support.** Should the group not reach consensus, revisit the back-up plan and confirm that everyone is willing to support the decision that comes out of it.

Caution   Coping with Time Crunch

If consensus can't be reached, don't leave the decision to move to the back-up plan to the last minute. Allow at least 10 minutes to reconfirm the back-up plan and the group's agreement to it.

6. **Recap and confirm.** Recap the decision and confirm consensus reminding members of the expectation that everyone support the decision and what that means.

   In order to test for true consensus, particularly on sensitive and important issues, it is important that the facilitator, having first reminded the group of the expectations attached to the word "support," check with each member. Ask specifically, addressing them by name, e.g. "Kathy, can you support this?"

Check for Consensus

Often a few vociferous individuals enthusiastically support an idea and others, who perhaps were earlier opponents, are now quiet. It can appear that these individuals have come to agreement. They may simply have been worn down or for some other reason have chosen not to register their disagreement. Other members, by their nature, may not be vocally giving their support to the decision. A few enthusiastic positive responses to the question, "Have we got agreement?" does not consensus make. Ensure that you schedule sufficient time to thoroughly check for consensus.

It is important not to rush consensus. On the other hand, groups often spend much more time in discussion than is necessary to reach consensus. Once you sense that all ideas have been heard and considered and members have focused on one or two options, ask whether the group is at a point where it can reach consensus. You might say "Are we at a point at which everyone can support one of these ideas?" Very often the answer is yes and a great deal of time is saved. If the answer is no, repeat the question periodically to both move the group along and to check where it is at.

Try This | Consensus Checks

 A quick visual way for group leaders to check the level of consensus is to ask members to put two thumbs up for "Yes, I like it!" or one thumb for "I can support it." No thumbs up indicates that "I'm not comfortable with it yet."

YOUR NOTES

Paving the Way for Consensus

In this section we have looked at the steps within the consensus process. The early steps described on The Meeting Map (Figure 1-1) are essential to consensus reaching. Although each step will have an impact on the group's success, clarifying objectives and establishing Meeting Agreements are essential.

Benefits of Consensus

The benefits of consensus that will help drive the decision forward to success include:

- Enthusiastic buy-in.
- The dialogue that is essential to the consensus reaching process results in better decisions.
- The thorough understanding of the issues that results from an effective consensus reaching process leads to more effective implementation of the decision.

Option 3: Majority Vote

The third option in making decisions as a group is by majority vote. Majority vote has potential downsides. It can be divisive and, if selected too quickly, may prevent beneficial dialogue.

However, it can be used effectively if an issue is not important, members have no strong preference, or if the number of options is limited and quite straightforward. In these instances, majority voting can be an important time saver.

Majority voting may also be used as an early step in consensus reaching in order to shorten the list of options. Multi-voting is a form of majority voting but when it is done well, it entails dialogue and is usually a step toward consensus.

Steps in Majority Voting

1. Clarify the group objective or problem to be resolved.
2. Review the options.
3. Confirm that the group accepts majority voting as the decision-making method.
4. Decide how the vote will be taken, for example, by a show of hands, colored dots on the flip chart, secret ballot, etc.
5. Determine what is a majority. For example, do three quarters of the members have to support the decision? See page 76 for more information on Multi-Voting.

Benefits of a Majority Vote

When used appropriately, a majority voting process has the following benefits:

- Majority voting is time-efficient.
- It is clear-cut and task-oriented groups often appreciate the decisiveness of it.
- When combined with good dialogue, it can work as effectively as consensus.

Becoming alert to decision-making potholes and learning how to avoid them can dramatically improve the decision-making process you lead. In this Chapter, we explored the three main ways to make good group decisions. Tools to further enhance problem-solving and decision-making sessions are explored in the next chapter.

YOUR NOTES

Decision Making Options

Option	Advantages	Potential Disadvantages	When to Use
One Person	• Quick. • Clear accountability.	• Low buy-in. • Insufficient understanding by group members to effectively support implementation.	• One person is the expert. • The group does not feel the need to share the decision (an opportunity to provide input to the decision may be appropriate depending on the degree to which the decision affects the group).
Voting	• Quick. • Clear outcome. • Quality decisions preceded by dialogue.	• Too quick/insufficient examination of decision options. • Winners and losers.	• Relatively unimportant item. • Everyone's buy-in is not required.
Consensus	• Full understanding. • High level of buy-in and support. • Strong follow through. • High quality/well considered decision.	• Requires consensus reaching skills. • Takes time.	• When a high level of buy-in is required. • When the decision is important and/or directly affects the team significantly. • When issues are sensitive.

Chapter 3

The Tools of the Trade

We have discussed the importance of structure in leading a successful meeting and have referred often to tools. The following are a set of problem-solving and decision-making tools that provide the structure and focus essential to reaching successful outcomes.

They include:

- The Generating and Organizing Ideas Technique
- Force Field Analysis
- Pros and Cons Chart
- Multi-Voting
- Priority Sequencing
- The Decision-Making Criteria Grid

THE GENERATING AND ORGANIZING IDEAS TECHNIQUE

The Generating and Organizing Ideas Technique, as outlined in Figure 3-1, was inspired by The Nominal Group Technique, a classic facilitation tool. The Nominal Group Technique was developed in the late 1960s by Andre Delbecq and Andrew Van de Ven as a program planning method (Justice, Tom and Jamison, David, *The Complete Guide To Facilitation* Amherst: HRD Press Inc., 1998). It has since become a tool that no meeting facilitator would leave home without. However, like most techniques that are used over time, variations have evolved and the technique is not always used well.

Figure 3.1: The Generating and Organizing Ideas Technique

1. **Clarification of the problem, objective or topic.**

2. **Silent generation of ideas.**

3. **Round Robin sharing of ideas.**

4. **Clarification and discussion of each idea.**

5. **Reaching agreement.**

6. **Commitment to action. Who will do what, when?**

The Generating and Organizing Ideas Technique responds to several questions commonly asked by meeting leaders, including:

- How can you get everyone involved?
- How can you prevent an individual in a more senior position from inhibiting others' participation?
- How can you increase the quality of the input or ideas?
- How can you prevent a few vocal people from driving the process and most strongly influencing the outcome?
- How can you keep the discussion focused?

It also provides structure that increases the effectiveness and efficiency of the group discussion and helps prevent conflict if the issue is sensitive.

The Generating and Organizing Ideas Technique offers you several options as to how ideas generated will be shared and collected. Members may share their ideas verbally, anonymously on a piece of paper to be read by the meeting facilitator, or on a sticky note which members will not share verbally but will stick on a flip chart or board.

Before beginning to work through the following steps, decide on the mode of participation that will work best for this meeting. If a number of members are highly uncomfortable speaking out in the group or if the issue is a sensitive one, which may inhibit participation, you may decide to have ideas put forward anonymously. This method of participation should not be used routinely. You must ensure that everyone is comfortable participating but, at the same time, must encourage open participation in which individuals contribute verbally and take ownership for their ideas. In today's organization, the ability to participate is a basic requirement and allowing people not to contribute verbally on an ongoing basis is not helpful to their growth or that of the organization.

If the group is able to share ideas openly, have all members put forward their ideas themselves.

A third option is a compromise between the two. Members write their ideas on a sticky note and stick it to the board. They take ownership for the idea by posting it, but don't have to share it verbally and are not asked to put their name on it.

YOUR NOTES

The Steps

Step1: Clarification of the Problem, Objective or Topic

Taking time to confirm understanding of what the group is setting out to accomplish is an essential first step. Without it, members may be working at cross-purposes or move off track. Post a concise statement describing the objective or, if appropriate, the problem definition. You will use these statements to ensure that everyone has a common understanding and to keep the discussion on topic.

Step 2: Silent Generation of Ideas

Invite members to quietly consider the issue to be discussed and to jot down their ideas. Where they write their ideas will depend on your choice as to the method of participation: their note pad if they are to share their own ideas; on identical pieces of paper provided by you if the ideas are to be turned in anonymously and read out by you; a sticky note if members are to capture ideas on paper and then post them to the board or flip chart.

Ask that these few minutes (five minutes is usually sufficient) be silent time. The silence allows everyone an opportunity to collect their thoughts. It prevents discussion of the topic allowing each member to engage in original thinking and also increases the quality of each contribution, as well as the likelihood that members will volunteer their ideas. If participants are inexperienced in the participation process, this preparation time can greatly increase their comfort level.

In addition, many more original ideas will be generated. When a discussion is unstructured and flows from a question such as "What are your ideas for … ?" the first people to speak influence the thinking of other members and can limit original thinking.

Try This	Build a Wall of Ideas

 Post blank sheets of flip chart paper around the room. Have each member choose a sheet of paper. Ask members to write as many ideas as possible on their sheet of paper.

Try This   Sticky Notes Increase Involvement

Most groups enjoy the sticky note method. Writing and posting the note increases their level of involvement in the process and the opportunity to get up from their seats and move around changes the pace and energizes the members.

Step 3: Round Robin Sharing of Ideas

Record ideas on a flip chart or board or so they can be projected (using a transparency or computer-generated slide). If members are presenting their own ideas, ask that they each present only one idea in the first round. This keeps the process moving quickly and prevents one person from presenting several ideas and perhaps leaving nothing for members further down the line to share. It has been noted that, even in seasoned groups, verbal participation at the idea generating stage increases ownership for the process and the outcomes.

Suggest members first present the idea or point that they feel most strongly about. If time permits, continue until all ideas have been shared.

Allow no discussion at this stage. Discussion of ideas now can lead to a too-early focus on one idea and perhaps premature decisions. If members are presenting written ideas anonymously, mix them up and ask a team member to record the ideas on the board or flip chart as you read them.

If members are writing their ideas on sticky notes, put a main heading on a board, usually the statement of objective or the problem definition and invite members to stick their notes below.

Step 4: Clarification and Discussion of Each Idea

Ensure that everyone has the same understanding of each point. Before discussing the ideas, review the group's statement of objective and/or definition of the problem. Ask members to keep these statements in mind as they discuss each idea.

Look for duplication and opportunities to combine any ideas. Don't allow combining of ideas without checking for understanding of the individual components to ensure they are expressing the same or very similar points. Combining ideas too hastily can cause the loss of important ones. If the process is not

YOUR NOTES

anonymous, check with the idea's originator before altering or combining. If it is anonymous still ask, "Does anyone feel we will lose anything by combining these two?" At this stage, members are often more comfortable participating (you have had time to demonstrate a safe environment) and are more likely to take ownership for their points.

Step 5: Reaching Agreement

If consensus does not fall out of the discussion, you might use one of the following tools:

- Multi-Voting
- Priority Sequencing
- The Decision Criteria Grid

all found later in this chapter. Chapter 2, Making Powerful Decisions, provides additional important information.

Step 6: Commitment to Action

This is the "where do we go from here" step. Ensure that the next steps are agreed to by everyone and captured as specifically as possible including *who* will do *what* and *when*.

Benefits

The Generating and Organizing Ideas Technique increases:

- The number of ideas generated.
- Participation in the discussion.
- The quality of the decision.
- The members' support for the decision as a result of full participation and a productive process.

Figure 3-2 provides a quick reference for options for generating ideas.

Caution	Judgmental Statements Inhibit

Discourage discussion at the round robin stage. Discussion at this stage can be judgmental, causing members to censor and possibly weaken their future responses. Even a positive comment such as "Great idea" is conveying a judgment. Members may shape future comments based on their perception of what group members will or won't like.

Figure 3.2: Options for Generating Ideas

Option	Method	Next Step	Benefits
Silent Generation of Ideas	Members write their ideas on notepad.	Round robin sharing of ideas.	• Increases participation. • Creates an opportunity for equal participation. • Increases the volume of ideas. • Allows for more carefully considered contributions.
Anonymous Generation of Ideas	Members write their ideas on a piece of paper which is given to the facilitator	The facilitator shares the ideas.	• Allows members to share ideas when a sensitive issue might otherwise limit participation (should be used rarely as members should feel free to express their ideas openly in most situations).
Building a Wall of Ideas	Blank sheets of flip chart paper are posted around the room. Each member chooses a sheet and writes as many ideas as possible.	The facilitator assists the group in identifying commonalities and combining the ideas into one list.	• Moving around is energizing. • Members have thinking time. • Members have the opportunity to contribute all of their ideas. • Creates a large volume of ideas.
Sticky Ideas	Each member is given large colored sticky notes, asked to write their ideas on them and post them under the topic heading posted on a board or wall.	The facilitator assists the group in identifying commonalities and combining the ideas into one list.	• Moving around and the visual effect of the sticky notes are energizing. • Large volume of ideas.
Pass the Envelope	Each member writes an idea on a piece of paper and puts it in an envelope. Each envelope is passed to another team member, that member writes an additional idea that is triggered by the idea in the envelope they received. They write it on a piece of paper and add it to the envelope. The process continues having each member examine all of the ideas in the envelopes they receive until each member has contributed to each envelope.	Ideas are sorted and compiled in a list (note: takes time).	• Volume of ideas. • Building on one another's ideas. • Encourages creative thinking.

FORCE FIELD ANALYSIS

Force Field Analysis is a golden oldie. It's used for idea and problem analysis and was first developed by Kurt Lewin in the early 50s but it is anything but obsolete.

Understanding the theory behind the tool enhances its use and sharing the knowledge with group members can increase their appreciation of its value.

Lewin suggested that any given situation, whether in an organization or in nature, is influenced by driving forces that propel a decision or event (a "change") forward to success. In contrast, restraining forces work against its success. Restraining forces attempt to maintain the status quo.

Lewin suggested that analyzing both sets of forces will provide insight into why something may not be working as we would have liked, as well as insight into how to move things forward.

He observed that when trying to bring about change through implementing a decision, it is our tendency to build up the driving forces. If the driving forces (the reasons why something is a good idea) are sufficiently strong, we believe that an idea will then work. However, Lewin observed that each time we create a driving force for change, a restraining force pops up to counterbalance it. The result? We often struggle to make decisions work.

Lewin suggested that we look at things from the opposite perspective. Instead of building up the driving forces, put greater emphasis on examining the restraining forces and finding ways to remove or lessen them.

In Figure 3-3, we use the example of a departmental restructuring. The fact that it is the president's idea is a strong driving force. However, there are restraining forces that may hinder the ease with which the restructuring happens. The budget is small which will limit the ability to make the physical changes that the restructuring would call for. People are happy the way things are. Everyone is busy, so finding the time to plan and make the changes will be difficult.

In this example, the group brainstormed to find ways to remove or lessen the power of the restraining forces. The actions they decided to take are described in Figure 3-3 under Strategies for Removing Restraining Forces.

Figure 3.3: Force Field Analysis

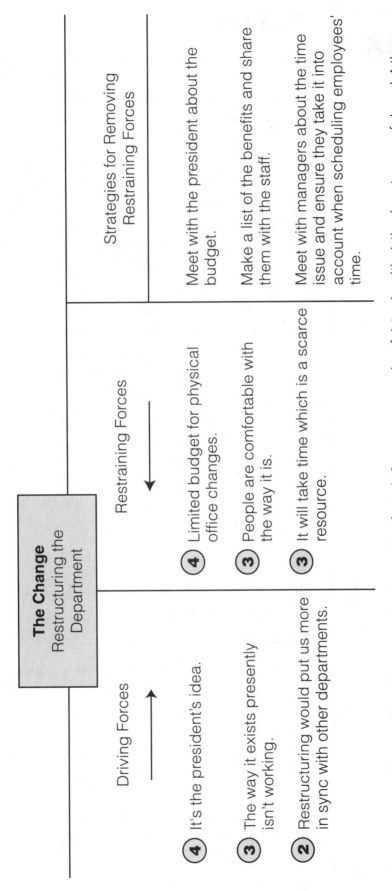

The Change
Restructuring the Department

Driving Forces

(4) It's the president's idea.

(3) The way it exists presently isn't working.

(2) Restructuring would put us more in sync with other departments.

Restraining Forces

(4) Limited budget for physical office changes.

(3) People are comfortable with the way it is.

(3) It will take time which is a scarce resource.

Strategies for Removing Restraining Forces

Meet with the president about the budget.

Make a list of the benefits and share them with the staff.

Meet with managers about the time issue and ensure they take it into account when scheduling employees' time.

Note: The numbers reflect the perceived power of each force on a scale of 1 to 4, with 1 the least powerful and 4 the most powerful.

YOUR NOTES

The Steps

1. Write the idea, proposed solution, or goal in the box marked "The Change" on your flip chart, board or lap top which has been set up like Figure 3-3.
2. Clarify the participants' understanding of the idea or goal.
3. Brainstorm to identify driving forces – situations, attitudes, personalities, resources – that support the change and record them.
4. Brainstorm to identify restraining forces – that is, anything that will prevent the change from happening or will hinder its effectiveness.
5. Have the group rank each driving and restraining force on a one to four scale; one being the least powerful influence, and four being the most powerful.
6. Encourage the group to assess the likely success of the idea or change by considering:
   (a) How powerful are the driving forces? Can we capitalize on the driving forces?
   (b) How powerful are the restraining forces? Can we manage or weaken them?
7. Decide whether the idea/change is workable.
8. If yes, develop strategies for removing or lessening the restraining forces.

PROS AND CONS CHART

Pros and cons charting is useful in comparing the potential effectiveness of different ideas.

The Steps

1. Select two to four ideas from your brainstorming list. If the group's list is longer, use the Priority Sequencing technique (page 77) to shorten the list.
2. Draw a Pros and Cons Chart on a flip chart or board, set up like Figure 3-4. Title the top box to suit your discussion, i.e. you might use simply Idea instead of Proposed Solution.
3. Write one of the solutions or ideas in the top box.
4. Invite participants to brainstorm to identify the pros and cons.

Figure 3.4: Pros and Cons Chart

Proposed Solution Develop a Web Site	
Pros	**Cons**
– Communicate with customers	– Time
– Sell products	– Cost
– Present a leading edge image	– Results can't be proven beforehand
	– Skills not available internally

YOUR NOTES

5. List the pros and cons without discussion as they are identified.

6. Discuss each. Put a pre-determined limit on the discussion time according to the number of options you are discussing. Allot approximately 10 to 15 minutes per option.

7. Follow the same procedure with each of the other suggestions.

8. Compare the charts of each idea. Which have stronger or more powerful pros and which have weaker or fewer cons?

9. Use this information to shorten the list of options.

10. Select a solution or idea as a group. A decision may be obvious at this point. If not, use the Multi-Voting method.

MULTI-VOTING

Multi-voting is a tool that organizes and increases the efficiency of the decision-making process. However, using the Multi-voting steps on their own does not ensure a good decision or one that is supported by all the group members. An open discussion of the various ideas being considered, comfort with the multi-voting method and an agreement that everyone will support the outcome are important before you begin the multi-voting process.

This method is used when the group has several options. Members are invited to indicate their preferences by placing self-adhesive colored dots beside their preferences which are posted for all to see.

The Steps

1. List the options that the group has identified on a flip chart or board.

2. Distribute colored self-adhesive dots to participants. One dot equals one vote. The number of votes each member will get depends on the length of the list. A general rule of thumb is that the number of votes each participant receives should equal 20% of the number of options on the list. So, for example, if there are 10 options, each person would have two votes and receive two dots. If there were 40 ideas listed, each member would have eight votes and eight dots.

3. Explain to the group that they can use their votes in any way they choose. They might put all of their votes on one or two choices or they might distribute them between several options on the list.

4. Allow approximately five minutes to weigh the options and distribute the stickers. If the group has more than ten members lengthen the time accordingly.

5. Count the votes and circle the 20% that received the most votes.

6. If the group is looking for more than one option, this could be the end of the decision-making process or:

   (a) You can repeat the process until you reach one choice,

or

   (b) You can move into a dialogue and consensus-reaching process using the new short list.

PRIORITY SEQUENCING

Priority sequencing is a variation on Multi-voting. This technique helps groups to come to agreement on the best idea or solution or to put the top ideas in priority sequence.

In the original design of the technique, members ranked their top favorite ideas, as many as five to nine, by assigning number values to each of their favorites – a rating of one for their top choice, two for their second choice and so on.

A simple method for achieving agreement and which also gets people moving around is to have each member choose their most favored and least favored idea. Each member places a green mark beside their favorite choice and a red mark beside their least favorite choice. It is easy to tally which ideas receive the most green marks.

Whatever method you choose, once you have identified the top choice(s), confirm consensus. Important—don't miss this.

THE DECISION-MAKING CRITERIA GRID

The Decision-Making Criteria Grid is a tool that helps the group make a choice by careful consideration of the criteria or requirements that will eventually determine whether the decision is effective.

YOUR NOTES

YOUR NOTES

Very often in decision-making processes, each member has their own undiscussed perception of what will make a good decision and why. This is one reason consensus is so often difficult to achieve.

Ensuring all criteria are shared with the group and accepted by all group members are essential steps in moving a group from emotional subjective-based discussions to objective-based dialogue, to achieving consensus and to making superior decisions.

The Steps

1. Set up a grid like the one in Figure 3-5 on a flip chart, board or computer-generated image. Confirm understanding of each option the group is considering and record each on the grid.

2. With the group, develop a list of criteria for selecting one of the options. You might use the Generating and Organizing Ideas Technique (Figure 3-1, page 66) to develop the criteria. Keep in mind that developing criteria is a decision-making process in itself, and depending on the complexity of the decision and the degree of cohesiveness within the group, this step can be quite time-consuming. If group members are not familiar with the concept of decision-making criteria, give examples of possible criteria. In the example, Figure 3-5 demonstrates the use of a decision-making grid for selecting a fund-raising event

    Or, as a catalyst for thinking, suggest that they answer the following: "How would you describe the best decision?" *or* "What are the important factors in making this decision?"

3. Record the agreed-upon criteria across the top of the grid.

4. Check with the group whether some criteria are significantly more important than others. A criterion might be weighted as twice as important or three times more important than others (described as 2X or 3X in Figure 3-5).

5. Explain the following scoring and decision-making steps with the group and check that there is full agreement with this decision-making method.

Figure 3.5: Example Using a Decision-Making Criteria Grid

Consider the degree to which each option fulfills each criterion and rate each criterion accordingly on a 1 to 4 scale.

1—Does not meet the criterion at all   2—Somewhat meets the criterion
3—For the most part meets the criterion   4—Fully meets the criterion

Criteria / Options	#1 Low cost	#2 Appealing to Target Market	#3 High Income Potential 3x*	#4 Little Manpower Required 2x*	Total
Dinner & dance	2, 1, 1, 2, 2 ÷ 5 = 1.6	4, 3, 3, 3, 4 ÷ 5 = 3.4	1, 1, 2, 2, 2 ÷ 5 = 1.6 × 3 = 4.8	2, 2, 2, 2, 2 ÷ 5 = 2 × 2 = 4	13.8
Casino night	3, 3, 3, 3, 3 ÷ 5 = 3	4, 4, 4, 3, 3 ÷ 5 = 3.6	4, 4, 4, 3, 3 ÷ 5 = 3.6 × 3 = 10.8	2, 2, 2, 2, 1 ÷ 5 = 1.8 × 2 = 3.6	21.0
Auction of goods from local merchants	4, 4, 4, 4, 4 ÷ 5 = 4	2, 2, 3, 3, 3 ÷ 5 = 2.6	3, 3, 2, 4, 3 ÷ 5 = 3 × 3 = 9	4, 4, 4, 3, 4 ÷ 5 = 3.8 × 2 = 7.6	23.2
Lottery	4, 4, 4, 4, 3 ÷ 5 = 3.8	3, 3, 3, 3, 2 ÷ 5 = 2.8	2, 2, 1, 3, 1 ÷ 5 = 1.8 × 3 = 5.4	4, 4, 4, 3, 3 ÷ 5 = 3.6 × 2 = 7.2	19.2
Auction of employees' services/skills	2, 2, 2, 2, 3 ÷ 5 = 2.2	3, 3, 2, 4, 3 ÷ 5 = 3	3, 3, 2, 2, 3 ÷ 5 = 2.6 × 3 = 7.8	2, 3, 3, 2, 4 ÷ 5 = 2.8 × 2 = 5.6	18.6

* Each of these was seen as more important (3 times and 2 times) and were weighted accordingly.

6. Members individually score each item against each criterion by ranking each on a one to four basis (four being high). If using weights, each score is then multiplied by the weight assigned to the criterion. (If you wish, you may provide each participant with a blank Decision-Making Criteria Grid sheet to work on).

7. All scores are collected and the average score recorded for each option under each criterion. Scores for each option are added and recorded under Total.

8. The group analyzes the totals and makes a decision based on which option has the highest score.

Benefits

Developing the criteria for the Decision-Making Criteria Grid helps focus the group's attention. Using the grid removes subjectivity and emotion from the discussion. Members are no longer able to cling to personal preferences. Whatever their feelings, the procedure forces members to consider the group's criteria and therefore to become more objective. In this way, the procedure facilitates consensus.

Developing criteria not only enhances the process, but directly impacts on the quality of the outcome by helping to ensure that no important factors are overlooked in the process. Often groups must revisit decisions because a lack of structure in the decision-making process has resulted in important factors being overlooked.

The Decision-Making Criteria Grid makes sense to most groups. It provides a deeper understanding of the rationale for the decision-making process and is seen as logical and fair. Therefore, buy-in is increased. Finally, the greater understanding of the rationale for the decision allows group members to better support it outside of the group.

The problem-solving and decision-making tools discussed in this chapter are the basic essentials that all meeting leaders should be able to use with ease. Each can be used for all types of meetings whether leading a short decision-making process at a regular team meeting or a full day problem-solving session.

Using the Tools for Problem-Solving and Decision-Making

Step 1   **Clarify the problem or the decision to be made.**

Step 2   **Generate ideas/solutions.**

Use:
• Generating Ideas Technique (page 65).

Step 3   **Analyse/examine the ideas generated.**

You might use:
• The Pros and Cons Chart (page 74).
• Force Field Analysis (page 72).

Step 4   **Make the decision.**

You might use:
• Multi-Voting (page 76)
• Priority Sequencing (page 77)
• The Decision-Making Grid (page 77)

Chapter 4

Performance Checks

The performance check is one of the simplest tools to use and yet along with Working Agreements, it ranks as the most important in your kit.

There are several types of performance checks, each designed to ensure that the factors critical to the group's success are not overlooked. Too often after a meeting, group members realize that important pieces were missing from their process with the result that the outcome or decision is not of as high a quality as the group is capable.

The various performance checks include:

- **The General Process Check.** If the members don't feel good about the way the meeting is working (the process), they are unlikely to contribute their best or embrace the outcomes enthusiastically.

- **The Logic Check.** Will the ideas work, are they quality ideas, were all factors considered?

- **The Feelings Check.** The ideas or decision might be logical, but how are people feeling? If feelings aren't addressed, good ideas may not be supported sufficiently to work well.

- **The Creativity Check.** Are the results "same old, same old" or has some innovative thinking taken place?

Each check focuses on a key meeting success factor.

YOUR NOTES

Caution   So Much To Do and So Little Time

Many of the process checks are not time-consuming, particularly the general process check, but the amount of time required depends on how well the team has met the success factor being examined. It's important to plan accordingly. If time is tight, determine beforehand which checks will be the most critical to the group's success and set aside time for them.

Usually five to ten minutes is enough. If, however, the group recognizes that the success factor being examined is weak or lacking, additional time may have to be devoted.

Alternatively, do a quick check with the group of each and make a call as to how much time can be dedicated to the particular check. This planning on the go takes more skill and can be handled best by seasoned meeting leaders.

Never eliminate the general process check.

THE GENERAL PROCESS CHECK

A General Process Check entails occasionally interrupting the discussion to check how well the group is working together to reach its objective. In a process check, you are checking to ensure that the members are feeling positively about the way in which the meeting has been going to this point. It gives you a reading on whether the choices you are making in leading the meeting have been on target, or whether you need to make some adjustments. It is so much better to learn about problems early on than to find out after the meeting that people were unhappy with the way it was led.

By using a process check, you also remind members of the importance of the process and their shared responsibility in its success. As they have been focusing intently on the task, the process or how they are working together may have been forgotten.

How well the process is working depends on a myriad of ingredients including the pace of the meeting, the headway the group feels it is making, the energy level of the group, the climate, the degree of participation, etc.

Be direct in using process checks. You might say: "Let's stop our discussion for a minute to do a process check to ensure that we are working together as effectively as possible." You might start with the wide open question, "How are we doing?" This usually generates discussion if there are concerns or if everyone feels things are working well the response is just nods or comments such as "great." If discussion has not been generated, probe further with a question like, "What would you like to change?"

Some groups may be uncomfortable giving direct feedback. They may be hesitant to appear critical of anything that they feel is your responsibility. Let the group know you are open to feedback by asking, "What can I do differently?" You may add specific questions related to facilitation judgment calls you have made particularly if you sense everyone may not have been equally comfortable. For example, you could try something like, "How is the pace? We have been working a little slower than usual because I sensed it was important to ensure that everyone understood the issue. Has this been working for you?"

This provides you with two opportunities: checking that everyone feels good about the way you are leading the group and helping the group to understand the rationale behind some of the calls you make, particularly the high risk ones. Note: this is not meant to suggest that you must explain every group process decision you make. However, if you sense some members are not in agreement with some of your calls, this can be an important step to getting them onside.

How Often Must You Check?

In a short meeting, perhaps an hour in length, use a General Process Check at least once during the meeting. In a full-day meeting, do several checks, perhaps just before each break. Process checks can also be added as needed.

Use a General Process Check when:

- You observe a behavior or dynamic that could impede the group's success. In this case, you would follow the initial step as described earlier: "Let's stop for a minute to do a process check to ensure that we are working together as effectively as possible." Add, "Is there anything we should be doing differently?"

  If the group doesn't identify the behavior or dynamic that concerns you, you might:

YOUR NOTES

– Refer back to the Working Agreements if the behavior you would like to address has been included there. "Do we need to pay more attention to our Meeting Agreements?"

– Describe what you have observed. When possible, do so without the use of names. For example, "I have observed that a few people are doing most of the talking." If the behavior does not change, you may have to become more direct.

• You would like personal feedback from the group on the way you are leading the meeting.

Benefits

The benefits of using the General Process Check include the following:

• As meeting leader, you receive frequent feedback allowing you to make adjustments along the way.

• Members are reminded of the importance of their behavior and interaction.

• Members learn that the success of the meeting is a shared responsibility and that it is not up to only the meeting leader to make it work.

• The facilitation skills a meeting leader brings to the process are often invisible to the group who are focused on the task. Often, the more successful the process, the less aware they are of the skills you bring. Process checks educate members on (or remind them of) the role of the facilitator, the thought that goes into the facilitation process and the skills required and used.

THE LOGIC CHECK

The Logic Check invites the group to pause and consider what they have produced to this point in the process. In this check, the group examines the content or task rather than the process.

A Logic Check might be introduced by the following statement, "Let's pause for a few minutes to check that we are on track to effectively meeting our objective." Do a quick recap of recommendations made, options presented, decisions made, etc.

Questions you might ask include:

- Have we missed anything?
- If we continue building on what we have produced so far, will we meet our objectives?
- How do these ideas meet the criteria?
- Does anyone have any concern that the decision we are moving toward will not fully solve the problem?

When structured decision-making processes such as the Decision-Making Criteria Grid are used, the time spent on logic checks will be greatly reduced, as it is less likely the group will have missed anything.

How Often Must You Check?

Logic Checks should be conducted twice in a meeting, although a long process may require more frequent use. Introduce a quick Logic Check as soon as a group starts moving down a certain path. Introduce a final check before the group makes its final decision. Also introduce a Logic Check if:

- You sense that the group's enthusiasm for an idea may have caused them to overlook important considerations. You need to ensure that nothing has been missed without dampening the group's enthusiasm.
- You recognize that the group is working on an assumption, rather than on known facts.
- You sense a gap in the group's logic. They have jumped to a conclusion.
- You recognize that the direction in which the group is headed will not result in their fulfilling the objective that has been set.

Benefits

The benefits of using a Logic Check include the increased likelihood that:

- The decisions made are of the highest quality.
- A more efficient group process results.
- There is better understanding and buy-in, as the decision and steps leading up to it have been thoroughly examined.

YOUR NOTES

FEELINGS CHECK

The Feelings Check, just as it sounds, checks how people are feeling. It is not, however, used to check how members are feeling about the process. That happens in the General Process Check. The Feelings Check is meant to give members an opportunity to express how they feel about the direction in which the discussion is going content-wise or the decisions being made.

Decisions may be logical, but in some instances members may still not feel good about them. People feeling poorly about a decision does not mean that that decision should not be made. The decision may be the best possible for the team and the organization. For example, someone might see the logic of a decision, but worry what it will mean for their job. Although often their concern cannot be resolved, providing an opportunity to express the concern and having others acknowledge it can help the member better deal with it and move ahead. (See Venting in Chapter 7, at page 110.)

In other instances when less than positive feelings are expressed, the group may find an equally effective alternative that makes people feel good as well. An example is a group is making a decision about what time of day to hold their meeting. A member feels left out because he or she needs to cover phones at the time the group has selected as the best time to hold meetings. In this case, the group could look for an alternative time that would work for everyone. Alternatively, the group may find a way to ensure that individual's input is taken to the meeting and output shared with him or her.

You might introduce a Feelings Check by saying, "Let's stop for a moment to check how everyone is feeling about the decision we are moving toward."

How Often Must You Check?

Check on the group's feelings at least once during a meeting. It is usually best positioned after a Logic Check, but not necessarily immediately after. Place it far enough into the process that the direction in which the group is heading is starting to take form or options have been developed, but not so close to the end of the meeting that there will be no time to make adjustments should they be appropriate. Also, use a Feelings Check anytime you sense any discomfort on the part of a member.

Benefits

The benefits of using a Feelings Check include the likelihood that:

- Members are more likely to fully support a decision if they know that their feelings have been heard and understood.
- The expression of feelings may move the group forward to an even better decision that not only meets all of the logical criteria, but also meets the members' personal needs. This is important, in particular, when the decision directly affects the members.
- There is a heightened awareness of members' feelings on an issue. Although the decision may need to remain as is, members may find ways to respond to concerns or feelings of fellow members.
- Consensus and full buy-in.

CREATIVITY CHECK

The Creativity Check asks members to challenge their thinking. Are they stuck in the old ways of approaching challenges? Are the solutions being put forward innovative enough to work in a highly competitive environment of fast-paced change?

If creativity is particularly important to the success of this meeting or if members are locked in old perspectives, consider some of the creativity tools recommended (Chapter 8, Get Innovative) as well as a brief Creativity Check.

In introducing the Creativity Check, briefly describe the need for innovation. If possible, tie it to something that is currently happening within the organization or team that highlights the need for innovation.

A generic introduction might be, "Few companies are succeeding today that don't recognize that yesterday's success means little and perhaps nothing. What was a good idea yesterday may be mediocre or even useless today. Innovative thinking is essential to success. So, how are *we* doing? Are we being sufficiently creative in our thinking?"

Or you could try some variation of the following statements:

- In what way are the solutions we have identified innovative enough to … (keep us ahead of our competition;

YOUR NOTES

keep up with our growth; meet the increasing expectations of our customers)?

- What have we put forward today that represents innovative thinking?
- In what way are the solutions we have developed today more innovative or forward thinking than those we would have put on the table two years ago?

How Often Must You Check?

It is always important that a group be aware of the need to think innovatively. However, some problems require more innovative solutions than others. If being innovative is highly important to the group's success, you may do a Creativity Check two to four times in a full day meeting. If not, one brief Creativity Check may be sufficient.

Introduce the Creativity Check at a point when the team is starting to move in a particular direction or beginning to formulate options or decisions. The Creativity Check works best after a Logic Check but does not have to be immediately afterward. It is most effectively used with additional tools from Chapter 8, Get Innovative.

In regular team meetings, usually an hour or two in length, depending on the agenda items, you may not need to do a Creativity Check at each meeting but ensure you use this check from time to time.

Benefits

The benefits of using a Creativity Check include the increased likelihood that:

- The group will make high quality, innovative decisions that work in today's competitive environment of change.
- The group members will become increasingly aware of the importance of innovative thinking.
- The group members will learn to recognize when they are, or are not, thinking innovatively.

Performance checks are designed to ensure that factors critical to the group's success are not overlooked. They may draw participants' attention to something they already know but are forgetting to use or may be catalysts for performance jumps.

A Quick Reference to Performance Checks

The Check	Purpose	Suggestions
The General Process Check	To ensure the meeting/group process is working well.	"Let's stop our discussion for a minute to check that we are working together as effectively as possible…"
The Logic Check	To ensure solutions that will work.	• "Have we missed anything." • "If we continue building on what we have produced so far, will we meet our objectives?" • "How do these ideas meet our criteria?" • "Does anyone have a concern that the decision we are moving toward will not fully solve the problem?"
The Feelings Check	To ensure that any member's feelings that could negatively impact the success of the decision are identified and addressed.	"Let's stop for a moment to check how everyone is feeling about the direction this decision is taking. Is there any aspect of this decision that you do not feel good about?" (Note: having already created a safe environment will be critical to people responding openly.)
The Creativity Check	To encourage innovative thinking.	"In what way are the solutions we have identified innovative enough to…(keep us ahead of our competition; keep up with our growth; meet the increasing expectations of our customers)?"

Chapter 5

Getting People to be Open to Ideas

Genuine listening is at the heart of every good meeting. Consensus can't be reached if people don't feel their ideas have been openly listened to; a group can't become synergistic, that is build on one anothers' ideas and take their discussion to the next level without being open to ideas; without receptivity to new ideas a group cannot respond innovatively to problems; good ideas are lost because they are ignored.

Structured decision-making methods such as the Generating and Organizing Ideas Technique (Chapter 3, page 65) encourage members to openly listen to one anothers' ideas. However, if too firmly held positions prevent flexibility and openness to new ideas, the group may need more help. Try one of the following dialogue opening techniques.

Caution Listening Fraud

One of the most difficult group types to facilitate is the group in which everyone understands appropriate group behaviors and so goes through the motions of listening, perhaps with head nods and "uh huhs." Everyone is polite, but no one makes any real effort to understand the others' opinions. In order to "unstick" this group, assertively introduce one of the techniques described in this chapter.

YOUR NOTES

Confirm Understanding

Members who are locked in positions usually believe that they understand the other point of view. Frequently they haven't listened carefully to what was being said, or they misunderstood. Confirming understanding is a quick way to check for understanding and quickly move the group ahead.

If the group has two or three members who see things very differently, ask each individual to describe his or her understanding of the others' ideas or points of view.

If the group is divided into two or more points of view, invite the most adamant members of each faction to describe their understanding of the others' point of view.

Switching Places

Invite members to consider the point of view opposite to their own and to develop two arguments for it. This works best if small groups of members work together to develop the arguments.

Recognizing and Setting Aside Assumptions

Group Assumptions

When the group as a whole appears to be stuck on one or more assumptions, try one of the following to break them out:

1. Use the first three steps of the Generating and Organizing Ideas Technique (Figure 3-1, page 66) to identify assumptions held by the group that pertain to the issue or topic being examined. Assumptions may relate to behaviors or attitudes (e.g., the purchasing people don't understand; management can't be trusted; people will never change), or they could relate to a technical issue. Experts often have strong assumptions shaped by years of looking at things from a particular perspective. These assumptions can cause a group to overlook good ideas because according to their assumptions, the idea could never work. For example, some companies missed the hype in the bottled water business because, in their experience, people bought beverages for their flavor. Therefore, water would never sell.

2. Once identified, discuss how the assumptions can limit dialogue and influence outcomes.

3. Ask group members what they can do to manage the assumptions. One possible response is to, "Give one another permission to bring members' attention to any behaviors or comments that suggest assumptions are being used. Add agreed upon responses to your Meeting Agreements (page 40).

Caution | Members Not Introspective

Identifying personal assumptions is a technique that works best with a group that has members who are able to self-examine. If members are highly rigid and unlikely to recognize their own assumptions, this exercise is unlikely to bring about dramatic change in this meeting. However, if you lead this meeting regularly, either as an inside or outside facilitator, using this exercise periodically can, over time, help members to see how their rigid thinking is limiting themselves and the group.

Personal Assumptions

Sometimes one or two members hold strong beliefs or assumptions that may be interfering with the group process. Try the following steps to help members better manage their own assumptions.

1. Invite members to identify assumptions that they personally bring to the issue or topic at hand. You might give them the following statements to spark their thinking:

   - I believe this group … (is not open to change; knows what's best).
   - I believe (the issue at hand) … (can never be resolved; has only one solution).

   Point out that you have used the word "believe" not "think." Assumptions are often dearly held, and disagreement with them is more likely to trigger emotion than logic. You may invite members to share their assumptions or you can also use this as an individual awareness raising exercise, where their responses are recorded on paper and not shared.

YOUR NOTES

2. Ask members to mentally set those assumptions aside during idea generation and discussion, so that they don't interfere with the members' ability to listen to others' ideas and make a powerful contribution to the meeting. Let them know that they are not being asked to permanently give up their assumptions or beliefs. In the final stages of decision-making, after having listened openly with no preconceived ideas, they can then decide if their initial assumptions are valid and useful in the decision-making process.

3. Ask members to give one another permission to bring attention to behaviors or comments that suggest an assumption may be getting in the way.

Acknowledge Feelings and Concerns

Group members can be stuck because of undisclosed feelings and concerns. Airing and dealing with them can help move the group along. Try the following steps:

1. Before beginning the examination of an issue or a consensus-reaching process, particularly if the issue at hand is sensitive, ask group members to sit quietly for a few minutes and reflect on what they are feeling and their concerns.

2. Invite members to share their feelings and concerns. Ask members to use the following rules:

   • No criticism or discussion of the comments, listening only.

   • There will be a pause between each observation to give members an opportunity to reflect on what has been shared.

   This should be a leisurely reflective process. Do not rush it.

3. Ask members to identify ways in which any negative feelings and concerns that have been identified could be lessened. Develop appropriate Meeting Agreements and add to your original list of agreements.

Achieving consensus is a goal of most groups, but groups cannot come to an agreement on an issue or solution if its members do not genuinely listen to one another. Setting aside assumptions, acknowledging concerns and confirming understanding are all part of genuine listening and of achieving consensus. Occasionally, group members may demonstrate additional difficult behaviors that we deal with in the next chapter.

YOUR NOTES

Techniques to Get People to be Open to Other's Ideas

Confirm Understanding

Confirming understanding of the different points of view should be a first step. Often people are not open to others' ideas because they weren't listening or the ideas weren't clearly enough presented. (Page 94)

Help Members Set Aside Assumptions

This technique requires that assumptions that may be limiting group or individual thinking are identified and set aside, at least long enough for members to openly listen to ideas. (Page 94)

Disclose Limiting Feelings and Concerns

Undisclosed feelings and concerns may prevent members from listening openly to ideas. Airing and dealing with them can open the group discussion. (Page 96)

Invite Members to Switch Places

This technique helps members to gain a better understanding of a point of view contrary to their own by devising arguments for that position. (Page 94)

Chapter 6

Dealing with Difficult Behaviors

In the next two chapters, we will deal with the challenges every meeting facilitator faces from time to time. The most dreaded challenges are non-productive behavior and conflict.

Here's the good news. Although it is essential to have tips up your sleeve should any of these situations arise, remember that a well-planned and well-facilitated process greatly reduces the likelihood of these arising. The more seasoned you become as a facilitator, the less often you will encounter any of these behaviors. Effective use of the Meeting Map and the tools we've discussed in earlier chapters will, for the most part, prevent the situations that create difficult behaviors.

TAPPING PEOPLE'S BEST

Most non-productive behaviors are not the result of someone entering the meeting room with the intent to sabotage. Most often, people demonstrating non-productive behaviors have a fear, a frustration, or a need that isn't being met. Individuals who demonstrate negative behavior in meetings most often aren't aware of how others are receiving their comments. They may not appreciate how their tone or behavior affects the meeting process.

The five behavioral styles following are most commonly identified as those hindering the group process.

YOUR NOTES

1. THE SILENT TYPE

These individuals are a challenge to the meeting leader's desire to ensure full participation. They may simply be quiet by nature or may have opted out of the process for some reason. Experienced meeting leaders can usually sense which is the case.

On occasion, meeting leaders focus so strongly on making everyone feel comfortable that they create an environment that does not challenge people to participate and so tap the best of themselves. It is important that all members feel secure, but are at the same time challenged to stretch themselves. If you anticipate that some meeting members will be silent types, specifically establish the expectation and importance of full participation at the outset. Add that you are not expecting that everyone will have the same amount of airtime, as everyone has a different personal style. What you are aiming for is that no one leaves the room with an idea that hasn't been expressed or a concern that hasn't been raised. Emphasize that expressing these things later, over coffee perhaps, will not be productive.

Be direct, but sensitive. If you sense that participating in a group is difficult or embarrassing for the individual, deflect the responsibility for their lack of participation away from them. For example, you might say, " You haven't had a chance to share your thoughts yet Kathy. What do you think?" rather than "We haven't heard from you yet."

If the group is sufficiently large, 10 or more members, and there are several people who are not comfortable participating, break the group into smaller discussion groups. Most people find participating in a smaller group easier than in a large one. It is also more difficult to opt out in a small group.

Reluctant participators are often more comfortable contributing to the discussion if they have had an opportunity to collect their thoughts. Some have simply fallen into the lazy habit of not participating because they regularly attend meetings in which participation is not an expectation. When inviting ideas, use the first two steps of the Generating and Organizing Ideas Technique, the silent generation of ideas and the round robin (as shown in Figure 3-1 at page 66). These steps give people time to develop an idea if they don't already have one and to think about how they will express it. Very importantly, by using these steps you communicate the expectation that everyone contributes.

For more information on how to increase participation see How Do You Ensure Full Participation? in Chapter 11 (page 147).

2. THE MONOPOLIZER

These individuals may have so much to say that it is difficult for others to contribute or they may have their own agenda that they are pushing. The root of monopolistic participation is often a positive one – enthusiasm. As meeting leader, you have to be careful to reduce that individual's airtime without dampening his or her enthusiasm.

In this case, be sure to acknowledge the individual's contribution and perhaps the level of enthusiasm and note that there are several other people whose ideas the group hasn't yet heard.

If the root of the overactive participant is simply an excessively talkative nature or the topic is a hot issue for someone, being direct works best. For example, try something like, "Mark, I need to interrupt you there. You have shared several – interesting/useful/creative (choose a word that acknowledges his contribution, but which is truthful, i.e. don't describe the ideas as useful, if they are not) – ideas, but there are several people whom we haven't heard from yet." Then turn immediately to someone else and invite that person's input.

When the monopolizer keeps repeating a point, it is usually because the individual doesn't feel he or she has been heard or understood. If the individual is a habitual monopolizer, the group often develops the habit of ignoring and not responding to that individual's comments. Often groups fear that any acknowledgement will encourage the monopolizer to continue. In actual fact, that response usually has the opposite effect. The monopolizer has no evidence that he or she has been heard and so continues to come back to the same point.

You might try this: "Ken, let me recap my understanding of what you are saying …" You might want to capture the key point on a flip chart as assurance that it will not be lost. Then ask, "Does everyone understand Mark's point?" It is likely that you will get some nods, then quickly continue, "Thanks Mark." Turn to another member and invite that person's input.

YOUR NOTES

YOUR NOTES

You may have to interrupt the monopolizer more than once before he or she changes his or her behavior.

3. THE INTIMIDATOR

The intimidator holds a strong position on an issue and presents his or her point of view very adamantly. They speak forcefully and may be judgmental, critical of others and tend not to listen. Their contribution may be emotional, expressing either anger or frustration.

Acknowledge their frustration, anger, or strong point of view, but emphasize that not everyone feels the way they do. Add that if the meeting is to be successful, every point of view must be expressed and equally considered.

If the intimidator does not change his or her behavior, point out more specifically the impact on the meeting. For example, "Carl, when you so adamantly insist that solution A is the only logical option, you limit the likelihood that people will openly support or explore option B. If we don't carefully explore both options, the quality of our decision-making process is put at risk. I understand your strong feelings on the issue. If you could participate productively in the examination of both options, in spite of your personal feelings, you would be making an important contribution to this process. Are you willing to do that?"

4. THE NICE GUY

This style is not obviously disruptive to the process but can limit the quality of the outcomes. The nice guy always wants to please everyone, is agreeable, hesitant to take a position and waffles.

Be direct. You might say, "Lee, I'm not sure I fully understand your position on this. What do you believe the best option to be?"

The nice guys can appear to agree in the meeting but may not be fully on board and may not wholeheartedly support the decision after the meeting. When a nice guy is present, it is doubly important that you take time to check for consensus. If the group is small, check for consensus with each member. If the group is large, ask the group whether anyone has any concerns about supporting the decision and check specifically with a handful of members including the nice guy. If asked directly if they fully support something and they say yes, the nice guy members are less likely to speak negatively after the fact.

5. THE UNHAPPY CAMPER

These group members present a negative attitude and often find fault with the process. Frequently, they simply do not want to be at the meeting.

If you have been able to manage or at least influence the meeting planning, every member should have been invited for a specific reason and should know why he or she is there. (See Chapter 1, under ensure the right people, page 17.)

If the individual has communicated a lack of interest in being there or the feeling that the meeting is a waste of time, it is likely that the importance of the meeting and the contribution that person can make has not been made clear.

Clarifying the meeting objective is an important step in getting unhappy campers to buy in. If that does not make a difference, clarify why people have been invited, either what the group as a whole has to offer, or better still what individuals, including the unhappy camper, bring to the table. You might get them involved and distracted from presenting negative behavior by asking them to take on a responsibility, for example, scribing, recording the group's ideas and decisions.

Use the working agreements and ensure that one agreement addresses the need to be positive. Remind the group of the agreements, and this one in particular, at the beginning of the meeting. Sometimes the unhappy camper realizes other team members are thinking of him or her when the agreement concerning attitudes is raised, and this may be sufficient to lessen his or her negativity.

If not, remind the individual directly of the agreement and ask for his or her support. This may not lead to positive, enthusiastic participation, but is likely to lessen the negativity.

If the individual persists in demonstrating behavior that is detrimental to the group moving ahead productively, acknowledge his or her discontent and ask that person whether a productive contribution to the process can be made feeling the way they do. If the answer is yes, it is likely they will make an effort to respond more positively. If the response is no (which is unlikely), it might be appropriate to free that individual from the process (if you have the power to do so).

If that person's inclusion or membership is not an option and the group will continue to meet on an ongoing basis, talk

YOUR NOTES

with him or her privately. Describe to the unhappy camper how his or her behavior effects the process; ask what you can do to assist them in making a more positive contribution to the group; ask for their support.

If the unhappy camper is a member of a regular team meeting and consistently presents a negative attitude, the behavior is likely reflective of a larger performance problem that cannot be solved by the meeting leader.

Dealing with difficult behaviors is a potential challenge for any meeting facilitator but a well-planned meeting has far less opportunities for such behaviors to present themselves. Understanding the five most common difficult behaviors prepares you, should they arise despite of the best laid plans.

Dealing With Difficult Behavior

Behavior Type	Occurs When	Try These
The Silent Type	Members do not participate.	• Highlight the importance of full participation with the entire group. • Use a Generating Ideas Technique. (page 65) • Invite their participation. E.g. "You haven't had a chance to share your thoughts yet Kathy, what ideas do you have?" • If the group has several Silent Types, break out into smaller discussion groups. (page 100)
The Monopolizer	A member dominates the discussion.	• Acknowledge their contribution and note that other's haven't as yet had the opportunity to fully express their point of view. Turn quickly to someone else. • Recap and perhaps record their main points to confirm that they have been heard.
The Intimidator	A member holds a strong position on a issue and presents it in a way that intimidates others and discounts their ideas.	• Acknowledge their position; emphasise that not everyone feels as they do. Add that if the meeting is to be successful every point of view must be expressed and equally considered. • If behavior doesn't change, be more direct. Describe the impact of their behavior on the meeting. E.g. "When you speak so adamantly, and dismiss others' ideas, some members may be hesitant to put forth ideas that may be critical to our success."
The Nice Guy	A member vacillates and doesn't take a firm position/agrees with everyone. May appear to agree in the meeting but not support the decision later.	• Be direct. Ask them to describe their position on the issue. • Check carefully for consensus. Ask them personally whether they can support the decision — look them in the eye.

Dealing With Difficult Behavior — continued

Behavior Type	Occurs When	Try These
The Unhappy Camper	Presents a negative attitude, may find fault with the process, may describe the meeting as a waste of time.	• Help prevent this by ensuring that the right people are invited, i.e. that everyone invited has something to contribute or gain. Ensure they are made aware of this before the meeting. • In the meeting clarify the objectives to ensure everyone understands why they are there. • Get the unhappy camper involved by giving them a role, e.g. note taker, time keeper, etc. • Use the Meeting Agreements (if the member is a perennial unhappy camper, it is likely that the group developed an agreement to help manage this type of negative behavior.) • Talk with him/her privately if they are an ongoing member of the team. • Describe to the unhappy camper how their behavior affects the process. • Ask if there is anything that can be done to have them feel more positively about the process. • If none of the above work, and if you have the authority, release them from the meeting.

Chapter 7

Dealing with Conflict

The common use of the word "conflict" suggests interaction that is negative by nature and is therefore something that must be avoided. Many people feel a great discomfort with conflict and make extraordinary efforts to avoid it. They are so adverse to it that they shut down any form of disagreement.

Not all conflict is negative. Differences of opinion, if well-facilitated, take the group discussion and the decisions that come out of it to a higher level.

As a meeting leader, you want to encourage different points of view. Groups whose members always agree may look efficient and compatible but they may be creating "group think," which means mediocre decisions or worse.

DETERMINING WHEN TO INTERVENE

One of the many decisions a meeting leader must make is whether to intervene when differences of opinion arise. Are members engaged in a high-spirited but ultimately healthy debate, or is the interaction dysfunctional?

Ask yourself whether the heated discussion is impeding the group's ability to meet its objectives. Consider the following:

- Are members attacking one another rather than the issue?
- Are some members uncomfortable with the nature of the discussion?
- Are good ideas or important perspectives not being heard because of the level of emotion? That is, are people not listening to one another?

- Is the group stuck on a heated issue that is preventing them from moving ahead?

   If you are not sure, do a process check. Stop the discussion and say something like this: "The discussion has become quite heated. Let's check whether the way we are interacting is productive or whether we need to approach the issue differently." Then invite the participants' observations.

Caution   Discomfort on the Sidelines

 A heated debate often involves only a few of the meeting members. It's important to closely follow the discussion and read the responses, both verbal and body, of those engaged in the exchange. But don't forget to also stay tuned in to those who are not participating. They may be experiencing more discomfort than the participants. If they feel threatened or uncomfortable with what is happening, it is likely that they will shut down or become less open for the rest of the meeting.

CONFLICT ARISES

If you carefully follow the Meeting Map (Figure 1-1) and make good use of the tools provided in *On Track*, it is unlikely that meetings you lead will experience negative conflict. Negative conflict arises most readily when the meeting discussion is a free-for-all, rather than a structured process.

- The objectives aren't understood and agreed upon.
- The group has no formal methods for managing the group process, e.g. meeting agreements.
- No facilitator is appointed (the group may believe they are experienced enough not to need one – often a pitfall.)
- Members allow personal assumptions to prevent them from listening openly.
- The group uses no formal decision-making processes or tools.
- The facilitator is not sufficiently skilled or assertive.
- Members have no skills in giving and receiving feedback.
- No process checks. The group does not interrupt its attention from the task to examine its process.

- Group avoids conflict; small disagreements are ignored until they grow into major issues.

PREVENTING NEGATIVE CONFLICT

The key steps to preventing conflict follow. More detailed how-tos are presented in other chapters, as noted.

1. Clarify the meeting objectives so that members aren't working at cross-purposes (Chapter 1, page 34).

2. Develop and use Meeting Agreements. As part of that process, invite group members to decide how they will deal with conflict should it arise and capture their decision in an agreement (Chapter 1, page 40).

3. Conflict often arises at the final decision-making stage. Define and get agreement at the outset as to how decisions will be made. If consensus is required, invite the group to adopt the following definition of consensus as a working agreement: *consensus is willingness to support the decision 100%*. Ensure discussion and clarification of the word support (Chapter 2, page 58).

4. Use structured problem-solving and decision-making methods. The more sensitive the issue, the tighter your structure needs to be. A structured approach minimizes emotion. It ensures that the group steps back and more objectively examines the problem. For example, using the Decision-Making Criteria Grid (Figure 3-5, page 79) forces the participants to focus on what the best decision looks like based on the needs of the team or organization, rather than their personal likes or dislikes.

   Other structured methods for problem-solving and decision-making include: Force Field Analysis (Figure 3-3, page 73), the Pros and Cons Chart (Figure 3-4, page 75), Multi-Voting (page 76), and the Generating and Organizing Ideas Technique (Figure 3-1, page 66). Determining when each is appropriate is discussed in Chapter 3, The Tools of the Trade.

5. Ensure full participation. In most instances, it is only a few members who bring high emotion to a discussion. They often monopolize the discussion and their emotion then fuels conflict. Ensure that everyone partici-

YOUR NOTES

pates and you will dilute the negative energy they are introducing.

6. Check for understanding of the points of view presented. Conflict often arises because of misunderstanding. When emotion is at play, one's hearing is often distorted. Paraphrase the key points: "Let's recap what is being said to ensure that we all have the same understanding."

7. Be assertive. Remember that you are the person who is ultimately responsible for the effectiveness of the process. Don't hesitate to intervene if you think the group may be heading for conflict.

WHEN CONFLICT IS PRESENT

In some instances you may not be able to prevent conflict. You may have missed an important early step or the conflict may have been carried, full-blown, into the meeting. In other instances, the purpose of the meeting may be conflict resolution and there is an acknowledged conflict that the group must work through.

Handle with Care	Venting Emotions

 If an issue is sensitive and feelings are running high, providing an opportunity for people to express their feelings can allow members to then set them aside and get down to the task.

You, however, must contain the venting process by limiting the time spent and prescribing parameters for the venting. For example, you might say, "I know this is a sensitive issue and many of you have strong feelings about what has been happening. I suggest that we take the next 10 minutes to express some of those feelings. Let's ensure that your feelings are described, but that no one is personally attacked. Our purpose is to express feelings and to better understand others' feelings, not to judge them."

Feedback Guidelines

Feedback guidelines help ensure that comments are made thoughtfully and with sensitivity. There is a danger that comments sparked by emotion may be careless. Some members may not know how to give feedback effectively.

Figure 7.1: Feedback Guidelines

Valuable Feedback:

- Is not given in anger.

- Describes facts (not perceptions/assumptions).

- Describes how you feel (if appropriate).

- Explains the reason for the concern (the impact or outcome).

- Allows for the other person's point of view.

- Suggests alternative actions if this is appropriate.

It is much easier to give valuable feedback if we expect it to be well received.

Being Receptive to Feedback Requires:

- Willingness to trust that the feedback is well intended.

- An understanding that feedback presents opportunities for growth.

- An ability to respond in a non-defensive manner. Non-defensive statements include: I hear what you are saying … tell me more … perhaps I could do it differently … do you have any suggestions.

YOUR NOTES

Present the Feedback Guidelines, as shown in Figure 7-1, and discuss them. Share the following:

- Receiving the feedback well is as important as giving it well.
- Feedback is best received when members trust that feedback is well meant, that it is given with the intent of making things better.
- The key to giving feedback well is to describe the facts or behaviors, not our perception of what happened. Rather than saying something like, "You let the team down" try "You didn't complete the follow-up by Monday, as you had agreed."

The first statement appears judgmental and the person receiving the feedback is likely to have an emotional response to it and disagree with it. The second simply describes facts. If they are accurate, the response will be less emotional and it will be more difficult for the person receiving the feedback to disagree.

If it is important to share the perceptions or feelings as well, add them after the facts are outlined. "You didn't complete the follow-up by Monday as you had agreed. The team felt that you had let them down."

Setting the Conflict Aside

If there is a strong difference of opinion that is impeding the group for the moment but the issue is not directly related to the group's objective, ask the group to set the difference aside. "It appears that you are not going to come to agreement on this point. My sense is that it is not necessary to agree on this to meet our objective. Would you agree?" Assuming the group agrees with this suggestion, continue, "I'm going to ask you to set that discussion aside and refocus on our objective for this meeting."

Leading the Group Through Conflict to Resolution

Your behavior and the tone you set strongly influence the course of a conflict situation. Ensure that you:

- Remain detached from the emotion of the conflict.
- Intervene assertively but positively when needed.
- Do not appear to take sides.

Try This | Lead by Example During Conflict

Model calmness. It is likely voices have been raised. Once you have the group's attention, lower your voice and slow the pace including your body movements. Perhaps sit down for a few moments to create a feeling of dialogue.

MANAGING CONFLICT

Some of the strategies for preventing conflict are also beneficial in managing conflict. For a quick reference on dealing with conflict, refer to the chart at the end of this chapter.

Revisit Meeting Agreements

In the event of conflict, it is likely that at least one of the original agreements has been broken during the conflict. Stop the discussion and ask the group whether they have been adhering to the agreements. Often the simple recognition that agreements have not been lived up to results in members taking ownership for their behavior and managing it more effectively themselves.

If a conflict causing behavior is present that has not been addressed in the agreements, ask the group whether any other agreements need to be added to the list. For example, they might add: "We need to agree to stop cutting one another off and really listen to what one another has to say." If group members do not recognize the negative behavior, share your observation.

Introduce a Process Check

Stopping the discussion and having the group step back briefly to observe its process also provides a cooling period, which usually removes the heat from the argument. See Chapter 4 for more details on process and other performance checks.

YOUR NOTES

While you must contain the emotion and negative interactions in order to resolve the conflict, you must also be careful not to shut down the discussion. Participants must feel free to express their points of view and the source of conflict must be addressed and resolved. There is a danger that the group can push the real issues underground and give the appearance of moving ahead. If this happens, it is likely that any decision made will be given only lip service by at least some of the members and will not have the required support to be implemented effectively.

Clarify Understanding

Ensure that participants understand each other's points of view. You might say, "Let's make sure that we all understand one another's points of view."

Invite one participant to recap his or her idea or perspective. Either describe your understanding of what the individual said or ask a member who is in conflict with this position to describe their understanding of what was said. Check for confirmation from the individual who owns the perspective.

Invite the other party to clarify that point of view and repeat the above step. If there are more than two perspectives, continue until they have all been recapped.

Once the points have been clarified, it is not unusual to discover that the perspectives are actually very similar.

Handle with Care   How Are We Feeling?

If emotion is high and the issue is sensitive or long-standing, it may also be beneficial to clarify the understanding of the members' feelings.

As in venting emotions, this must be carefully handled. Position it and provide parameters. You might say, "In order for the group to move forward, it is important that everyone understand each other's feelings. How someone else may have reacted to the situation may be very different from you. Keep in mind that feelings are neither right nor wrong. Our purpose is not to dispute the feelings but to acknowledge and better understand them."

Check the Group's Readiness to Agree?

Once you have used one or more of the interventions described earlier, check whether the group is now ready to come to agreement. Disagreement is often not the result of substantive differences, but of poor communication and misunderstanding. Once all members know that their point of view has been listened to with respect and has been understood, the group is often ready for resolution.

When Differences are Substantive

The conflict may not simply be the result of misunderstanding and emotion but there may be substantive differences. Clarify these points of view and diffuse the emotion and then invite the members to suggest a resolution.

When Conflict is About the Decision

When conflict arises in the decision-making process, introduce a decision-making tool such as The Decision-Making Criteria Grid from Chapter 3 (page 77). You should also refer the members to the consensus agreement.

Chapter 2 outlined the importance of working toward consensus and having everyone agree to support the decision 100%. Refer to this agreement from time to time during the discussion. You might say, "There are still some differences of opinion but are we at a point where everyone can support this option?"

Often members are ready to agree but would continue a heated discussion if allowed to do so.

Build on Common Ground

Post the heading "Options" on the flip chart or lap top and list the different suggestions below it. Add the heading "Benefits" and identify the benefits each option provides. Look for the common ground. All options are likely to present many of the same benefits. (See Figure 7-2 for a sample of this tool.)

Continue with the heading "Needs Not Met" and identify what is perceived to be missing in each option.

The common ground under the "Benefits" is usually much greater than the differences noted under "Needs Not Met." Point this out to the group.

YOUR NOTES

Figure 7.2: Build on Common Ground

Option	Benefits	Needs Not Met	Solution that Maintains Benefits & Meets Needs

Ask, "Is there a solution that will ensure that all of these needs are met?" You may suggest that the group build on one of the options already listed (check Chapter 8, Get Innovative). Group members may respond with a compromise solution.

Caution	Avoid Mediocre Decisions

 Obtaining a compromise can be a positive approach to resolving conflict providing the quality of the decision is not effected. Any compromise solution must provide the same benefits (i.e., meet the criteria for the decision) and must be one that people will support. Too often, groups are satisfied if everyone says they can live with it. "Living with it" doesn't suggest any commitment to making the decision work.

THE ROOTS OF CONFLICT

When conflict is difficult to resolve, inviting the group to examine the roots of the conflict can be useful.

- Introduce the group to the roots of the conflict (see Figure 7-3). Describe each of the roots of conflict.
- Ask the members to identify which of the roots apply to the conflict they are experiencing. Discuss these roots and how they have caused the conflict.
- Invite the group to decide how it can manage these underlying issues. Confirm that if these issues are managed, the conflict will be resolved.

Figure 7.3: The Roots of Conflict

The Roots of Conflict
The following are the most common causes of group conflict.

Different Values
As our organizations become more diverse and open, they become more complex. Values are shaped by many factors including, profession, culture, background and lifestyle. As corporate cultures are becoming more open, people are feeling freer to bring their values into the workplace — values which used to be left at the door when they entered the workplace. In a decision-making process, a myriad of values may directly or indirectly come into play.

Different Agendas or Priorities
Different agendas or priorities may be acknowledged. In a cross-functional team, for example, members from the finance department, quality control and human resources are likely to each have different priorities that could come into play in a decision-making process.

In other instances, there is one acknowledged agenda but other hidden agendas.

When everyone is not aiming for the same outcome or are using different, undiscussed criteria in the decision-making process, consensus is unlikely and conflict very likely.

Different Workstyles
Different workstyles can lead to conflict. Consider these opposites — detail oriented and big picture oriented; people who prefer to work most comfortably with logic and those who depend on interaction; those who like to bring things to closure quickly and those who like to open up discussion and mull things over. The opposites in each pair can approach aspects of a group process very differently, sometimes leading to frustration and often conflict. The group can benefit from the differences if the differences are acknowledged, discussed and the group recognizes how they can benefit from the strengths each style brings to the process.

Miscommunication
Miscommunication often results from assumptions being made about the intent or meaning behind what someone said or didn't say or even their body language.

Dealing with Conflict

To Prevent Conflict
- Clarify the meeting objectives to ensure members aren't working at cross-purposes.
- Discuss how conflict will be handled should it arise and create appropriate working agreements. (Page 40)
- Get agreement on how the decision will be made. If consensus is selected, define it as *willingness to support a decision 100%.*
- Use structured problem-solving and decision-making methods. (The more sensitive the issue, the more structure that is required.)
- Ensure full participation.
- Check for understanding of the points of view presented.
- Be assertive, don't hesitate to intervene if you think the group may be heading for conflict.

To Manage Conflict
- Do a process check. (Page 84)
- Provide an opportunity to vent emotions. (Page 110)
- Introduce the Feedback Guidelines. (Page 110)
- Set the conflict aside if not relevant to the group's objectives. (Page 112)
- Remain objective (don't take sides).
- Revisit the meeting agreements related to conflict or if no appropriate agreement exists invite the group to add agreements that will manage conflict.
- Clarify understanding of the opposing parties' points of view.
- When the conflict is related to the decision-making process, use decision-making tools from Chapter 2.
- Remind the group of the consensus definition *willingness to support the decision 100%.*
- Build on common ground. (Page 116)
- Help the group find a compromise that will allow them to effectively meet their objective.
- If conflict is deep rooted, work through the roots of conflict. (Page 118)
- If differences are substantial, facilitate the group in problem-solving to find a resolution.

Chapter 8

Get Innovative

Innovative ideas have always distinguished the good from the mediocre and the exceptional from the good. In times of fast-paced change and heightened competition, innovation becomes even more critical.

Although there is a difference between the dictionary definitions of innovation and creativity, we will use them interchangeably here.

The tools and tips *On Track* has given you this far will ensure efficient and effective meetings. Using these methods will maximize the chance that groups will meet their objectives and make strong decisions that everyone fully supports. People will leave meetings with the "That was a great meeting!" response. This section gives you the tools and information to take groups to the next level where they experience breakthrough thinking.

Breakthrough thinking happens in groups when:

- The meeting space and set-up are conducive to innovative thinking.
- Activities that trigger creative thinking are introduced.
- Creative thinking is an expectation. Members of most groups (those whose job it is to be creative do not fit this norm) spend most of their time using logic.
- Members are reminded to think innovatively.
- Members are able to engage in risk-free and productive dialogue.

- The environment is safe for creative thinking. No one fears sounding foolish.
- Idea generation and discussion are structured to tap members' creativity.

ENVIRONMENTS THAT SPARK CREATIVE THINKING

The physical environment is seldom neutral. It either stimulates open, creative thinking or it stifles it. Some simple strategies make a difference.

It's harder to come up with new ideas in the same old place. If the group meets regularly, change meeting rooms as often as possible. Ask members to refrain from sitting in the same seat or beside the same individual at each meeting. If there is only one choice of meeting room, change the set-up. At the very least, hold important meetings off site. The extra cost is well worth it.

Also try the following hints to spark creativity:

- If the meeting is longer than one or two hours, ask members to change seats partway through.
- Choose a casual meeting space and set-up. Easy chairs and sofas work well if the group is small.
- For larger groups arrange huddles of six to eight people in circles.
- Look for rooms with windows. Natural lighting has a strong impact on the energy level of the group. No energy, no creativity.
- Use brightly colored markers and slides.
- Put toys on the meeting tables or put fresh flowers in the room (be careful of allergies).
- Play music at breaks or have it playing quietly in the background throughout the meeting. If trying the latter, check with the group. Some people find it stimulates their thinking, some find it distracts them.
- Have colorful posters related to the meeting theme or topic.
- Use your own creativity to identify ways to create a stimulating environment.

Too often little thought is given to the impact of the meeting environment on the process. Make this a priority.

STARTING OUT RIGHT

We discussed earlier (The Meeting Map, page 32) the benefits of starting meetings with an energizing activity. In meetings in which you plan to tap creativity, these are essential. You might use brainteasers (Energizers 1 to 4 in Worksheets, pages 203-210), riddles or any type of activity that requires members to break from their usual thought pattern.

Try This | Increase Creativity

 If you wish to increase creative thinking in regular team meetings, ask members to take turns bringing energizers or brief games to the meeting.

TOOLS FOR TAPPING CREATIVITY

Using the following tools and techniques will support you in setting an expectation of creativity, establishing a safe environment, and structuring the process to best tap the members' creativity. Figures 8-1 through 8-3 at the end of this chapter provide guidelines on some great tools for getting teams thinking innovatively.

The most commonly used tool to tap creativity is the Brainstorming Technique.

The Brainstorming Technique

The Brainstorming Technique is designed to encourage creative or "out of the box" thinking. Use it when a new, innovative idea is particularly needed or if the group tends to be rigid in their thinking. This can be a limbering up exercise for the mind. However, if helping a group change their thinking style is your purpose for using the Brainstorming Technique, don't be discouraged if the results aren't initially as creative as you would have hoped for. A highly structured, task-oriented group often takes a little longer to "get into" brainstorming. With a group that demonstrates a highly logical mindset, change is seen if the brainstorming techniques, along with other activities presented in this chapter, are used on a regular basis. Post or distribute Figure 8-4 at the outset of the exercise.

Figure 8.4: Rules for Brainstorming

- **Bizarre ideas are welcome.**

- **Look for opportunities to build on ideas.**

- **Do not evaluate or discuss ideas.**

- **Everyone participates.**

- **Produce as many ideas as possible.**

- **Throw out ideas quickly.**

- **Have fun.**

Steps

1. Clarify the topic or problem. Post it where it can be seen.

2. Present and get agreement on Figure 8-4, Rules for Brainstorming. For example, you might say, "In order to ensure that we brainstorm effectively, I am going to ask that you each keep some brainstorming rules in mind:

   - Bizarre ideas are welcome. (Our intention is to think in new ways.)
   - Look for opportunities to build on each others' ideas.
   - We will not evaluate or discuss any ideas until all ideas are out.
   - Everyone participants.
   - Produce as many ideas as possible.
   - Throw out ideas quickly. (We want this to be a fast-paced activity.)
   - Have fun.

3. You might set a timeframe for idea generation. Five to ten minutes is an average time spent by teams in throwing out the ideas. The time required is affected by the size of the group and level of creativity.

4. Invite members to throw out their ideas. Encourage members to put them forward as quickly as possible. Capture each idea on a flip chart or board as it is presented. Don't worry at this point about your penmanship or the artistic nature of your chart. The priority is to create a fast-paced, energetic process.

5. Encourage ideas to continue to flow until the time limit expires, if you have set one, or until ideas begin to come very slowly. It's like preparing popcorn in a microwave. The popcorn is done when the time between the pops becomes extended.

6. Provide five minutes of reflection time to allow members quietly to consider the ideas. This reflection time often produces even better ideas or opportunities for building on ideas.

7. Add additional ideas to the list.

YOUR NOTES

YOUR NOTES

8. Discuss the ideas. Ensure that everyone has a common understanding of each one. Look for commonalities and opportunities for combining ideas.

Watch for the likely headnods once the group is into the discussion, people start putting their logical hats back on. Logic, of course, is necessary to identify ideas that will work, but don't let members dismiss any ideas too quickly. Challenge their thinking, particularly on ideas that people like, but that they don't see as being feasible. You might say, "On the surface, this may seem like an idea that can't work. Let's take a few minutes to explore how you could make it work."

9. Agree on the best ideas using Multi-Voting, Priority Sequencing or the Decision Making Criteria Grid (see Chapter 3).

Try This	Give Quotas

When brainstorming, give the group a large idea quota. Having to produce a large number ensures members won't eliminate ideas before they share them. The first ideas that come out will be standard, reflecting the usual thinking of the group members. As they stretch further to meet the quota, ideas become increasingly original.

Benefits

The Brainstorming Technique increases:

- Group creativity.
- The number of ideas generated.
- The level of participation in the discussion.
- Group energy.
- The quality of the outcomes.
- The participants' support for the decision (as a result of full participation and/or a productive process).

Setting Assumptions Aside

Assumptions stifle creativity. If members assume certain things are a given, their idea generation will be limited. How to get groups to set assumptions aside is discussed in Chapter 5, Getting People to Be Open to Others' Ideas (page 93).

Look for "That Won't Work" Treasures

Great ideas are often buried under the surface of ideas that appear to be unworkable. The most creative ideas often don't conform with members' usual way of doing things or thinking. Don't allow ideas to be dismissed too quickly.

Suggest that the group consider the idea a little longer. Use one or both of the following tools.

1. Looking For the Gold

1. Challenge members to think of themselves as a group that has been charged with the task of making this idea work.
2. Ask members to jot down ideas for modifications that would improve the idea.
3. Invite them to share their ideas round robin fashion and capture the ideas on a board, flip chart or electronically.
4. Examine the modifications and ask the group to decide whether continuing to work on the idea would be worthwhile.

2. Removing the Obstacles

1. Invite the group to identify the aspects of the idea that they think make it unworkable.
2. Examine each of the perceived obstacles. Ask the members to address two questions:
   - "Is it a fact that this is an obstacle, or is it our perception that this is an obstacle?" Ask members to substantiate their answer.
   - "Is there anything that can be done to remove this obstacle?"
3. Ask the group to decide whether obstacles can be removed sufficiently to make the idea workable.

Force Field Analysis (Figure 3-3 , page 73) can also be used to examine ideas that might seem unworkable.

Tapping Group Intuition

The group owns a body of knowledge that goes beyond the collection of information and experience that are most readily turned to when making decisions. The group also owns intuitive knowledge. Too often the group, absorbed in facts and rushing

YOUR NOTES

because of time pressure, misses this less obvious but highly valuable knowledge. Accessing this knowledge is particularly important when innovative thinking is required and important decisions are being made. For a great exercise using reflection time to its utmost, see Figure 8-5.

Reflection Time

Groups need more reflection time. In a recent survey on innovation, 47% of managers identified time pressures as the number one factor limiting innovation.

Reflection is a quiet time in which the group stops its discussion and ideally moves away from the table and preferably out of the room for a few minutes. Members put thinking aside and check how they are *feeling* about the options or decision before them. It is also a time to give the thinking process a break by letting the mind wander. Reflection is particularly critical if the decision is an important one or difficult to reach.

When Should Reflection be Introduced?

Introduce reflection after the group has shortened its list of priorities or before it makes its final decision.

Steps

1. Tell the group that you would like them to take a reflection break before they make their decision. Explain that moving away from the discussion for a few minutes can be important in ensuring the best decision.
   Ask them:

   • To move away from the table and, ideally, out of the room.
   • To not talk or check messages. Emphasize that they are still in the decision-making process.
   • To stop *thinking* about the decision for a few minutes and check how they are *feeling*.
   • To let their minds wander over the decision.
   • Then let their minds wander away from the topic for a few minutes.

   Allow approximately 10 minutes. If the decision is very important, you might allow more time.

Figure 8.5: Time for Reflection*

This idea generating process lasts over approximately a four-week period providing time for thoughtful reflection and building on one anothers' ideas.

1. Provide each participant with a notebook in which you have written the problem definition or objective.

2. Instruct each participant to write at least one idea per day in his or her notebook for one week.

3. Provide participants with different color pens or fine line markers. Colors stimulate the creative process.

4. Have participants exchange notebooks at the end of the week. Ask members to use the ideas in the notebook they receive to trigger as many new ideas as possible. The different color ink helps to highlight the building process.

5. Continue the exchange for four weeks, collect the notebooks, summarize and categorize the ideas.

6. Facilitate a group discussion of the ideas that emerge from the process.

* This technique was inspired by the Notebooks technique from *Crunching Creativity* by Michael Michalko.

3. When they return, ask first how they are feeling about the options or the decision. Do they still feel that the direction in which they are headed is correct?

4. Ask whether any thoughts came to anyone that they would like to share. (Often when the mind wanders from the topic, ideas and thoughts surface that would not have, had the group continued to discuss.)

5. Return to the decision-making process. Under some circumstances, "sleeping on it" has validity. If the decision is very important and time allows, consider breaking and reconvening the next day. This should be the exception, not the norm. There is an urgency to get decisions made and implemented and leaving decisions from one meeting to the next should not become a habit.

Tapping Individual Members' Intuition

Stay alert for the individuals who are most tuned into their intuition. These individuals can sometimes be recognized by their use of phrases such as "I sense" or "I have a feeling." Probe their thoughts to check that the group isn't missing any important insights.

Innovation often does not just happen, but it is sparked by highly effective meeting facilitators.

Figure 8.1: Wordy Brainstorming

1. Describe the problem or objective.

2. Provide the group with a jar full of random words. Put each word on a colored piece of laminated paper. All words should be nouns/objects.

3. Invite the group to draw three or four words.

4. Place each word selected on the top of a flipchart.

5. Invite the group to brainstorm for characteristics of the object. For example, if the word were briefcase, the group might say:

   • It's portable.

   • Comes in different sizes, shapes and materials.

   • It opens.

   • It carries things.

   • It can be locked.

   • There are different styles for different people or uses.

6. Make the connection. Force the group to look for connections between the briefcase and possible solutions to your problem. You might ask, "How is the briefcase like the ideal solution to our problem?" or "Which briefcase characteristic could also be characteristics to the solution of our problem?"

   For example, if the problem is "We can no longer afford to fly all of our sales people to head office for the product launch."

   Perhaps the briefcase characteristic "it's portable" would trigger thinking about taking mini-product launches to each region.

   "There are different styles for different people or uses" might trigger the idea that the mini-launches could be designed to highlight the new product features most important to a particular region.

Figure 8.2: Picture It

1. When problem solving, break the group into smaller work groups — ideally three to six people.

2. Ask that they draw something that reflects the current situation or problem. For example, in a team building session: "Draw an animal that reflects the characteristics of your team today."

   Then ask them to draw the ideal, for example, "Draw an animal that reflects the team you want to be."

3. Invite each group to present their pictures and the characteristics each represents.

4. Examine each characteristic and brainstorm to identify ways to move from the current state to the ideal.

Figure 8.3: Brain Writing

1. Clarify and post the problem or objective.

2. Distribute large index cards.

3. Invite participants to each write an idea on a card and pass the card silently (no discussion) to the person on their right. Ask them to write large enough to be readable from a few feet (cards will eventually be taped on a wall).

4. Instruct the members to read the cards passed to them and write down build-ons or new ideas inspired by them. Allot 20 minutes for this part of the activity.

5. Collect the cards and have group members tape them to a wall.

6. Invite members to gather around the posted cards. Ask the group to look for categories of ideas.

7. Write category headings and stick them to the wall. Move the cards under the appropriate headings.

8. Clarify understanding of the ideas.

9. Distribute colored dots and use the Multi-Voting Technique (page 76) to select the top ideas.

Check Your Meeting Leadership Style

Becoming more aware of your meeting leadership style can take your facilitation skills to a whole new level.

Each meeting is a mix of two types of behaviors: task-oriented behaviors focusing on the content (what is discussed and what is decided) and process-oriented behaviors focusing on how the group works together. Task-oriented is a heads down, "let's get to business" style. Process-oriented is a heads up, "let's look around" style. Figure 9-1 gives examples of both types of behavior. You will see that they are polar opposites.

Our personal styles are also a mix of task orientation and process orientation. Meeting leaders often don't recognize the fact that they lead the meeting according to their personal style and preferences.

If you are highly task-oriented, you may have a tendency to push things ahead too quickly without sufficient discussion; you may focus more on the content than the people and miss important signals from the members. It is possible that you'll ensure the group checks the details, but you may allow them to miss the bigger picture issues. On the upside, you are likely to ensure an efficient, organized process; you will bring items effectively to closure and ensure commitments to action are attached to each; and you will keep the discussion on track and on time.

If you are highly process-oriented, you might let discussions continue for too long; let discussions wander off track; not

Figure 9.1: Task/Process Balance

Task-Oriented Behaviors	Process-Oriented Behaviors
Telling	Asking
Focusing on details	Focusing on the "big picture"
Keeping on track	Taking the discussion on side trips (not always a bad thing)
Working and thinking independently	Working with others and sharing ideas
Using logic	Using creativity and intuition
Bringing things to closure	Opening things up
Focusing on the topic/content	Focusing on the people and group interaction
Focusing on what is decided	Focusing on how a decision is made

Note: These are generic task-oriented and process-oriented behaviors and do not apply only to meetings.

challenge members' behavior for fear of hurting people's feelings; or hold the facilitation reins too loosely. On the plus side, you are likely to bring to the meeting leadership role the ability to tune into people and read their body language; an ability to set a comfortable environment; and a commitment to ensuring that everyone's point of view is heard and understood.

Most people demonstrate a mix of task behaviors and process behaviors. Some individuals are "natural" group facilitators as their preference for task and for process is balanced. They work as comfortably in one mode as the other and move easily back and forth between the two. They instinctively recognize when to focus on task behaviors (e.g. dotting i's and crossing t's, using logic, bringing things to closure) and when to emphasize process behaviors (e.g. checking how people are feeling, encouraging participation, sparking creative thinking).

However, being predominantly task-oriented or process-oriented by nature doesn't prevent someone from being a highly effective meeting leader. It does mean, however, that they benefit from recognizing and managing their natural tendencies to ensure that they bring their strengths to the meeting leadership role without the potential weaknesses.

Consider whether you tend to demonstrate either task-oriented behaviors or process-oriented behaviors more prominently when leading meetings.

CHECK YOUR TASK/PROCESS STYLE

If you are predominantly task-oriented by nature, you will likely:

- Do careful meeting planning.
- Provide structure.
- Keep the discussion on track.
- Pay attention to detail.
- Bring items to closure.
- Ensure commitments to action.
- Finish on time.

You may also:

- Not get sufficient input from the group in the planning process.
- Move the discussion along too quickly.

YOUR NOTES

- Provide the answers without letting the group work through them.
- Slip into the discussion/content.
- Re-word and change the intent of participants' input when recording the ideas.
- Miss members' body language.
- Not check regularly for consensus.

If you are predominantly process-oriented by nature, you will likely:

- Develop creative meeting plans.
- Effectively read the mood of the group.
- Ensure full participation.
- Be sensitive to members' body language.
- Create a comfortable environment.
- Check for consensus regularly.
- Encourage creative thinking.

You may also:

- Not provide sufficient structure.
- Not pay attention to detail.
- Allow the discussion to wander or to continue too long.
- Allow the participants to too strongly influence the process design or structure (i.e., do your job).
- Not be assertive enough in managing non-productive behaviors.
- Not bring the discussion tightly enough to closure.

Meeting leaders who increase their awareness of their task- and process-oriented behaviors increase the effectiveness of the meetings they lead.

To achieve an effective balance between the two, you might set aside time after meetings you lead to reflect on the meeting and assess your performance. Reflect on the leadership behaviors discussed above and identify those you demonstrated during the meeting. Did those behaviors increase the effectiveness of the meeting? What would you do differently next time?

Ask a meeting member to act as your coach. Provide them with a copy of the Task/Process Balance notes described in Figure 9-1 or the list provided above. Ask them to share with you the behaviors they noted you using during the meeting.

Learning to use the meeting tools presented in earlier chapters is a relatively easy task. Changing your personal facilitation style is a little bit more difficult, but can ultimately help you move to the next level where you will facilitate even more effectively with even greater ease.

YOUR NOTES

Chapter 10

The Essential Skill

QUESTIONING—A CRITICAL SKILL

The questions you ask the group members during the meeting are critical to the success of the meeting. Questions can move the discussion forward, challenge and expand members' thinking, ensure understanding and quality decisions.

Asking the right questions requires:

- Understanding the questioning process and the options available to you.
- Preparation and understanding of the group's core issues.
- Being highly tuned-in to the group and the discussion.
- Learning from experience.

Types of Questions

Questions fall into two broad categories, closed and open-ended questions.

Closed questions require only a short, one word or phrase answer, often a yes or no. In effective meeting facilitation, closed questions are used sparingly and only for specific information gathering. As they suggest, closed questions close down discussion. They usually begin with "does," "can," "is" or "how many." Examples include:

- "Does everyone agree?"
- "How many people will be at the meeting?"

YOUR NOTES

Open-ended questions elicit responses that are more thoughtful and detailed. They can be built on by other participants; they move the discussion forward. Examples of open-ended questions include:

- "How do you feel the managers should respond to the situation?"
- "What ideas do you have for improving the system?"

Track the type of questions you use. Do you miss opportunities to move the discussion ahead by misusing closed questions? For example, "Was that a good decision?" is a closed question that will likely receive a yes or no answer. Think about why you are asking a question and use an open-ended question that will get you a thoughtful answer. Turn closed questions into open ones. Instead of "Was that a good decision?" you might ask "What did you like or dislike about the decision? Let's start with the likes."

In order to ask questions that will move the group toward its objectives, you must:

- Use questions purposefully.
- Know how to phrase the question.
- Listen actively to the response.
- Respond effectively to the answer.

Try This	Review, Reflect and Reuse

 Shortly after the meeting while the details are still fresh in your mind, review the process. Reflect on the questions you asked, the responses you received and where the questions led the process. Would you now word any of the questions differently?

Use Questions Purposefully

You may use a question to:

1. **Gather information.** Questions may gather information:

   - Related to facts. These may be closed questions. For example, one closed question could be, "How many people responded to the survey?"

Figure 10.1: Using Questions Purposefully

Purpose	Examples
To Gather Information – related to facts – related to feelings	 How many people responded to the survey? How do we feel about the proposal that is being made regarding the new Customer Services System?
To Probe – for understanding – for more in-depth information	 Can you tell us more about ...? Why do you believe that to be the case? What else could be done about it?
To Challenge Peoples' Thinking	What assumptions might be limiting the ideas put forward? If money were no object, what solutions might you offer?
To Increase Participation	Who can build on Ken's point? Who has a different point of view to offer? What other ideas can you add?
To Probe for Sensitive Information	Some people feel management has not been listening? What is your feeling?

- Related to feelings. For example, this open question might be posed, "How do you feel about the progress that is being made on the new customer service system?"

2. **Probe for understanding and more in-depth information.** Questions probing for greater understanding of an issue may include the following:

- "Can you tell us more about … ?"
- "Why do you believe that to be the case?"
- "What else could be done about it?"

3. **Challenge people's thinking.** Questions which challenge assumptions and jump-start creativity include:

- "What assumptions might be limiting the ideas put forward?"
- "If money were no object what solutions would you offer?"

4. **Increase participation.** Encourage group participation through questions such as:

- "Who can build on Ken's point?"
- "Who has a different point of view to offer?"
- "What other ideas can you add?"

Figure 10-1 provides a quick reference of questions with a purpose.

Phrasing the Question

Be clear and concise in your phrasing of all questions. No rambling. Your questions are meant to keep the group focused and move them ahead.

Be sensitive to individuals and the group as a whole. Word questions positively without diluting the issue to be tackled. For example, instead of asking, "How are you going to fix this mess?" try "What can you do to turn the situation around?"

Responding to Members' Answers

Listen actively to the response to your question. Make eye contact with the person responding. You might encourage the member to give more detail by prompting, "Tell us more about … "

If the issue is sensitive or complex, check your understanding of the answer by paraphrasing what the person said. "Let me check my understanding. You are concerned that … "

Do not judge what the group members have to say but ensure that they know you understand and appreciate their contribution. Your responses could include simple statements like:

- "Thanks for sharing that."
- "Thanks, Ken."
- "I understand what you are saying."

You can also acknowledge the contribution by building on it. For example, you might try, "Let's see if we can build on Ken's point. What might you add?"

Try This   A Question Coach

 Invite a team member to be your question coach. Ask them to jot down each question you ask, who responds, the gist of that response and where that leads the discussion. Discuss their notes and observations with them after the meeting. Track how each question influenced the discussion.

Asking questions is easy. Asking questions that spark stimulating, effective meetings and exceptional outcomes is an art – one that can be learned with practice.

Chapter 11

Common "How Do You ...?" Questions

This chapter is meant as a quick reference guide to answers to the most common "How do you?" questions asked by meeting facilitators. Some of the information was presented in earlier chapters but is organized here under a particular meeting challenge. Much of it is new.

Meeting leaders with excellent facilitation skills often identify one challenge that they would like to be able to handle more effectively. One small, easy-to-apply tip or technique can make the difference. This chapter offers a large selection to choose from. It is unlikely you will choose to use all of them. Find those that best fit you and the meetings you lead.

HOW DO YOU ENSURE FULL PARTICIPATION?

A multitude of variables collide in determining the degree of participation in a meeting. Your personal style, the personal style of each meeting member, the tools and techniques you choose to use and how you use them, together determine whether there is full participation.

There are a number of tools and techniques during both the planning and the course of the meeting that will increase your success level and ensure full participation.

1. Do Your Homework

If you are an outside facilitator you will have to gather more information than a facilitator who is also a team member. If you are leading a meeting of your own team you will already have the answers to the questions below.

YOUR NOTES

In either case, think about the answers to the following questions. Ask yourself questions like: "How might that affect the meeting process? What can I do to capitalize on the strengths and contain or lessen any of the difficulties?" Draw on the techniques provided in the earlier chapters and in the following "How to" sections.

In your pre-meeting information gathering meeting with the group, determine the following:

- Do group members have experience in participatory meetings.
- Are some members quiet by nature?
- Are any members likely to dominate the discussion?
- Will managers be present and, if so, might they affect the level of participation?
- Have there been major changes or stressors in the organization that might affect how people feel when they come into the meeting?
- Are the topics to be discussed sensitive? Is there any history attached to the topics that could affect participation?
- What kind of a track record does the organization have on listening and following through on employees' ideas?
- Is there any conflict between group members that could come into play in the meeting?
- If the group has worked together in the past, did the members do so effectively?

2. Use a Participation Survey

If the group or several of the members have met together before, gather information on the level and quality of participation in previous meetings. Note that you might do this even if you have been part of those meetings to check that your perceptions of the participation at the meetings is consistent with that of other members. Distribute the Participation Survey (Figure 11-1) to each member. Explain that you will be using the responses to ensure an effective meeting. Have each member complete and return it to you before the meeting.

The results of the survey provide you with important information about the group. Completing the survey ensures that members begin to think in advance about the importance of

Figure 11.1: Participation Survey

Consider your group's meetings and respond to each of the following statements by rating it on a scale of 1 to 4:

1 – Does not describe us at all.

4 – Describes us all of the time.

1.	Everyone participates in our meetings.	1	2	3	4
2.	Some members participate more actively than others.	1	2	3	4
3.	Some members more strongly influence outcomes.	1	2	3	4
4.	We experience conflict in our meetings.	1	2	3	4
5.	We make decisions easily.	1	2	3	4
6.	Members readily raise concerns.	1	2	3	4
7.	Members contribute ideas and solutions.	1	2	3	4
8.	Members receive feedback well.	1	2	3	4
9.	Members give feedback well.	1	2	3	4
10.	Members leave our meetings feeling positive.	1	2	3	4

participation and their usual behaviors. The responses can also be used in the meeting when developing Meeting Agreements.

3. Develop a Relationship with the Group

Begin laying the ground work for a good working relationship before the meeting. If you do not know the group members, send out a pre-meeting note introducing yourself and telling them that you are looking forward to working with them in the meeting. If you already know the group members, add a personal note to any pre-meeting material you send out.

If the topic to be addressed is a sensitive one and the group is not too large, meet one on one with members before the meeting. The primary objective of these meetings is to ensure that you have the background information you need. However, a huge spin-off benefit is that the members have an opportunity to begin to get to know and trust you.

Chat with members before the meeting as they enter the meeting room.

4. Model Openness

Respond openly to questions about the meeting that members may have. Model openness during the meeting and, as appropriate, share your own experiences.

5. Open with a Meeting Energizer

Open the meeting with a short activity that is fun and requires everyone's participation. Often referred to as ice breakers, meeting energizers do that very well. They quickly increase participants' comfort with one another and with participating in the group. See the Worksheet section at back of this book for different meeting energizers you can use. For an endless supply of meeting energizers, check out *Brain Teasers for Teams Leaders* (McGraw-Hill Ryerson, 2000) or visit ***www.lbendaly.com***.

6. Keep the Group Energized

When energy lags, so does participation. Humor is an energy generator, as are quick team activities such as brainteasers. Try inviting the group to stand up and stretch or lead the group in one or two easy aerobic exercises.

7. Establish the Expectation that Members Participate

Members may attend information sharing meetings or meetings in which participation is not an expectation. Meeting members with this experience frequently see their responsibility as limited to simply showing up and contributing only if they choose to.

State clearly at the outset that in order for the group to effectively meet its objectives, full participation is essential. Clarify full participation as, "No one leaving the meeting with an idea they haven't expressed or a concern they haven't raised." It does not mean that everyone will necessarily have the same airtime. If you anticipate less than full participation in the meeting, allow the group a few minutes to discuss the need for full participation and how it can be achieved.

8. Choose Tools that Structure the Participation Process

Choose from the tools in Chapter 3, such as The Generating and Organizing Ideas Technique (Figure 3-1).

9. Develop Meeting Agreements that Support Openness and Participation

When developing Meeting Agreements (Chapter 1, page 40), it is likely a team member will suggest: "We must agree to be honest and open." Once you have agreement on this add: "Everyone agrees that honesty and openness are important to our success today. What else do we need to agree to make it safe or comfortable for members to participate openly?"

Resulting agreements are likely to include, "We agree not to take comments personally" or "We agree that comments made in this room are held in confidence."

The development of the Meeting Agreements is as important as their use. Developing them allows the members to raise concerns about participation that might have prevented them from being open had they not been discussed.

10. Address Perceived Repercussions

If members are concerned that there could be repercussions if their comments are seen as negative, it is likely you will uncover this in your meeting preparation work. It may be appropriate to speak in advance with managers or leaders who will be part

YOUR NOTES

of the meeting and prepare them to address it at the beginning of the meeting. If the manager's behavior in meetings has been interpreted in the past as defensive or aggressive, you may need to coach them.

Suggest they take care not to respond too quickly or adamantly. When receiving critical feedback, the rationale for decisions, if presented too quickly can appear defensive. When receiving suggestions, explaining too quickly why they won't work will shut down the group.

The greatest challenge for many strong managers is to pause, reflect, and probe for more information rather than immediately reacting to comments from the members.

For some parts of the discussion, it may be appropriate for the manager to leave and let the group work on its own. The group must be prepared, however, to share the key points of discussion with the manager. (See also How Do You Deal with Senior People in Meetings, page 156.)

11. Ensure Common Understanding

Clarify understanding of the topic or the group's objective. This should be done via pre-meeting communication and revisited at the beginning of the meeting. Lack of clear understanding inhibits participation.

12. Develop Group Ownership for the Process and Outcomes

People are more likely to participate in something that they see as their own. Share any information that shows how group members have contributed to the setting of the objectives and the topics to be discussed. This includes sharing survey results or information collected in one-on-one meetings (not, of course, sharing the names of those who shared the information unless that was agreed upon).

With the heavy work schedules most people experience, meetings are often seen as an additional burden. Take time to discuss:

- Why this meeting/why this topic?
- What will the organization gain?
- What will meeting members gain?
- Why is it important that these members be part of this process?

The amount of time devoted to this discussion depends on the degree of resistance within the group. If lack of buy-in to the meeting process is a serious issue, consider breaking into smaller groups to discuss the above points to ensure everyone has an opportunity to contribute to the discussion.

13. Make It Easy

Make participation in the group meeting as easy as possible, particularly for those who are not confident participating in a group. Use the Silent Generation of Ideas and the Round Robin methods (from the Generating and Organizing Ideas Technique, Figure 3-1, page 66).

The Silent Generation of Ideas allows members who may not be confident putting forth ideas, time to collect their thoughts. Using it also ensures that all thinking and participation styles are accommodated. Many people make their greatest contribution when they have had time to collect their thoughts quietly. A freewheeling discussion inhibits their thinking and without the quiet reflection time, such individuals often cannot contribute their best. Those who produce their best when stimulated by the interaction with others will have this need met later in the discussion.

The Round Robin relieves quieter members of the onus of trying to find an opportunity to speak. Everyone is invited by name to contribute.

If the issue is highly sensitive and several members find participation difficult, you might invite the group to write their ideas down and hand them to you to be shared. Use this method only in unusual circumstances.

14. Break Out into Smaller Groups

Try breaking the group into smaller groups. It is easier for most people to share ideas with a few people. In addition, from a time perspective, it allows each person more airtime. Circulate to check that the less assertive members' ideas are not getting lost and that they will be represented in the final reports back to the larger group.

Breakout groups can be of any size, but ideally will have no more than eight members. On some occasions, it might be appropriate to create groups of only two or three people for more in-

YOUR NOTES

YOUR NOTES

depth or intimate discussion. In most cases, five to eight people works well, as there are enough people to create synergy.

For breakout groups to work effectively, they require a **discussion facilitator**. The quality of discussion within the breakout groups is as important as that within the larger group. Introduce the Meeting Success Factors as shown in Figure 11-2 and emphasize the importance of each factor in the quality of their discussion.

15. Be Direct

If someone is not participating fully, invite them to by name.

Try This	Give Them Warning!

When inviting quieter members to participate, make it easier by preparing them rather than suddenly asking for their ideas. You might say: "We haven't heard everyone's ideas yet. Who else has something to add? How about you Sim? What have you been thinking about?"

This allows the quiet group members to prepare as you have signaled that you are likely heading in their direction. Asking "What do you have to add?" often leads to the easy response, "Nothing." The more open-ended question, "What have you been thinking about?" is likely to elicit a more thoughtful response.

16. Help People Come Prepared

Ensure members know why they are there and what they are expected to contribute to the meeting. Communicate this in meeting notifications. The Vital Agenda (Figure 1-7, page 22) is a tool that ensures everyone understands what is being discussed and how they can prepare for the meeting.

Make sure any briefing notes are sent out far enough ahead to allow the members to read them thoroughly. Keep pre-reading material as short as possible.

17. Acknowledge and Build on Participation

Acknowledge each participant's contribution by capturing ideas on a flip chart or board. If a comment is not relevant to this discussion, place it in the parking lot (Chapter 1, page 37) to be handled later.

Figure 11.2: Meeting Success Factors

To ensure the success of your breakout group, please make sure that each of the following steps occur:

- Appoint a facilitator.

- Assign roles such as scribe, time keeper and spokesperson.

- Clarify the task or objective. (What have we been asked to do?)

- Keep the discussion on track.

- Ensure full participation.

- Keep on time.

- Get agreement.

- Recap.

Listen intently to everyone's comments. Responses such as, "Thanks for sharing that" may be appropriate.

Build on members' ideas with encouragement such as: "What can you add to Simon's suggestion?" Even if the idea is "off track," show appreciation for the participation. For example, you might say, "Thanks Susan for getting us started. Who can add an idea?"

Try to find something in "off-track" ideas that can be used as a bridge. If someone suggested, "Let's just fire everyone," you might say, "Martin is suggesting the need for a fresh start. What ideas do you have that would help the group start fresh?"

18. Deal with Behavior that Might Shut Others Down

Use the dealing with difficult behaviors techniques in Chapter 6.

19. Add Lightness

Humor, used appropriately, is useful even in the most serious discussions. People who laugh together can work together much more effectively. Humor balances the mood of the meeting and can prevent members from taking things too seriously. Humor can take the form of anecdotes or fun energizers. Don't miss the opportunity to learn about and build on group history, including the inside jokes.

HOW DO YOU DEAL WITH SENIOR PEOPLE IN MEETINGS?

The two most common concerns about senior people in meetings is that they may inhibit participation and they may drive the decisions. Often that senior person is the manager or leader of the group, so they can be a daunting presence. There are a number of ways to manage this situation.

Caution	Shift the Perspective

Often meeting facilitators, particularly inside facilitators such as a team member who may be leading a meeting, are uncomfortable dealing with senior people in meetings. The facilitator sees it as a problem resulting from a particular leader's style and therefore a sensitive issue. Instead, develop the mindset and approach that it is common for group processes to be strongly influenced by a leader's comments and responses. Therefore it is simply good meeting practice to address the issue, it is not a reflection on a particular leader's style.

1. Discuss with the Senior Person Before the Meeting

Clarify with the manager what role he or she intends to play in the meeting. Clarify the level of empowerment at which the group is expected to work.

Levels of Empowerment

1. **The manager/leader makes the decision.** If working at this level (no empowerment), the manager will be presenting a decision to the group.

2. **The manager makes the decision with input from the team.** In this case, the manager will be presenting an issue or problem to the group for discussion and the manager will be taking away the members' input to be used in the decision-making process.

3. **The manager and team make the decision together, with consensus.** In this case the manager has knowledge and experience that are valuable to the decision making process but the team members have equally valuable knowledge and experience. All members, including the manager, will equally influence the decision.

4. **The group makes the decision without the manager.** In this case, the manager is not part of the discussion. However, depending on the nature of the decision, it may be important for the manager to establish decision-making criteria with the group, such as budget parameters. If the manager has any input or information to offer the team, ensure that this happens before the team begins the decision-making process. It shouldn't be nec-

essary for the manager to be present for the decision-making.

Ensure the level of empowerment is clarified with the group in the meeting.

2. Coach the Leader

Leaders seldom intend to unduly influence a meeting but may not be sensitive to the behaviors that can create negative impressions and how they may be perceived by group members. Suggest approaches that the leader might use to present their points of view and to avoid the situations outlined below.

On the Attack

The very characteristics that contribute to a leader's success can hinder their effectiveness in meetings in which they are perceived to be the most powerful individual. Their high energy and directness can come across as an attack.

A leader may be seeking more information when they shoot back a response to a comment. However, questions like "What do you base that on?" or "Give me an example" can be perceived as a challenge to the comment, rather than a sincere probe for more information. This type of response is a discussion closer. Instead, something like, "I think I hear what you are saying but help me make sure I understand. Can you give me an example?" keeps the discussion open.

On the Defensive

When receiving input, the manager's best response is simply listening in a way that lets people know they have been heard. That might include nodding, jotting down notes or simply looking at someone and saying, "thank you."

Very often a leader feels the need to immediately explain why things had to be done a certain way. Giving this explanation immediately can create the impression of defensiveness or unwillingness to change. If it is important for the leader to provide an explanation, ensure that the members have been sincerely listened to first.

First at Bat

When the leader puts forth his or her ideas early in the discussion, it can inhibit others' contribution. There may be the perception: "Well, that's obviously the way she wants it." Or there may be a reluctance to present ideas that don't conform to those of the leader. Ideally the leader's ideas are presented somewhere in the middle. Last at bat is also not ideal as it can suggest "the final word."

3. Increase Your Confidence

If you, as the facilitator, are concerned about having to manage the participation of a senior person, give yourself permission by effectively using the Clarify the Role of the Meeting Leader step of the Facilitation Map (Figure 1-1, page 38). For example, try a statement like, "In order to work together effectively to meet our objectives, I may ... (describe three or four actions you might take in facilitating the discussion, include whatever you are most uncomfortable doing, e.g. asking some individuals to give others more air time, etc.)." It is easier to take whatever action you need to when you have already declared the possibility and people are expecting it as part of your role.

4. Address the Issue Upfront

Acknowledge the fact that having senior people in a meeting can sometimes affect the group process. Open this for discussion and recommendations at the beginning of the meeting. Often this leads to good suggestions as to how the group can best benefit from the presence of the leader, rather than being inhibited. Even if members do not openly respond, it is likely the leader will. At the very least, the leader has been reminded of the influence he or she can have.

5. The Right Meeting Agreements

When developing the group's Meeting Agreements, you might ask whether the presence of senior people could in any way hinder the group's process and invite any suggestions for Meeting Agreements (see Chapter 7, page 113) to deal with the possibility.

HOW DO YOU USE A TIMED AGENDA?

We have all attended meetings that have had too much on the agenda. The group may rush through each item, suggesting that the intent of the meeting was to simply be able to stroke each item off the list; thoroughly discuss the first few and sprint through the remainder; or simply run out of time and not address, perhaps important, issues.

YOUR NOTES

Having to commit to a time for each item on the agenda means that appropriate meeting management decisions are made at the planning stage. If the time required for each item adds up to more time than has been scheduled, there are some obvious options – lengthen the meeting or cut out some items. That weeding process can be a healthy one. Which items are the most important? Can some of the items be dealt with in another fashion? Perhaps they pertain to only a few members and can be handled by them outside of the meeting. Could staff members looking for input receive it by e-mail?

Managing Time During the Meeting

Keeping track of time allotted to each agenda item assists the facilitator in ensuring the group achieves its objective in the allotted time and, perhaps even more importantly, can be used to help keep the group focused. If, for example, you have allotted 20 minutes for a particular item, ten minutes has already passed and the group is in a discussion that is unlikely to get the group to its objective within the remaining time, point out how much time is left and ask: "If we keep the discussion very focused, can we effectively reach our objective in ten minutes?" Frequently, the answer is yes and members simply needed a reminder to keep focused and move ahead.

If the answer is no, then determine how lengthening the time spent on that item will affect the rest of the agenda and how the group will deal with it.

Rather than asking the group how they will handle the fact that their agenda will now run overtime, present a recommendation. For example, you could say something like: "The last item on our agenda is not urgent. I suggest that we move it to our next meeting. That will give us an additional 15 minutes. Do you think that will work?" It is likely that you will get agreement if your recommendation is a reasonable one.

If instead you invite a discussion of how to deal with the now too long agenda, you could end up using more of the group's limited time non-productively.

For an example of a timed agenda, see the Vital Agenda, Figure 1-7, page 22.

HOW CAN YOU BEST FACILITATE A MEETING WHEN YOU ARE THE TEAM LEADER OR A MEMBER?

There is seldom an advantage to having the leader facilitate a meeting of the team they lead. The exception is if none of the team members have meeting facilitation skills. Often the leader facilitates the meetings simply because this is the way it has always been done.

Having someone else lead the meeting has many advantages. The leader has an opportunity to sit back and reflect on the topics at hand and the input from members and can more easily make contributions themselves. Being both a stakeholder and meeting leader always presents the challenge of balancing the role of objective facilitator with that of a member who has opinions and ideas to share. Doing so as a leader is doubly difficult.

The ease and success with which a leader can facilitate a meeting of their own group depends primarily on three things:

1. The team's climate.
2. The sensitivity or importance of the issue.
3. The leader's style.

1. Team Climate

A positive team climate means there is a feeling of well being within the team. There is a sense of honesty, openness and trust. People do not fear repercussions from sharing their opinion and therefore will not be inhibited if the leader is facilitating the meeting.

2. Sensitivity of the Issue

The greater the sensitivity of the issue, the more difficult it may be for the leader to facilitate the meeting.

3. Leadership Style

A *facilitative style* inside and outside of meetings greatly strengthens a leader's ability to lead their group's meetings. A leader with a facilitative style is able to create open dialogue. The leader shares his or her point of view and encourages people to stretch their thinking but does so in a style that communicates:

YOUR NOTES

YOUR NOTES

- "I am listening."
- "I value your ideas."
- "I am not judging you."

A *directive leadership style* communicates (usually unknowingly):

- "I am right." (Therefore you are wrong.)
- "I am on the defensive." (Prove your point.)
- "I am driving the decision." (My way or no way.)

Figure 11-3, Can the Leader Effectively Lead the Meeting?, offers some scenarios that are helpful.

Leaders with directive styles often don't recognize their own behavior and how it affects the group. They must face the challenge of setting aside their personal preferences and opinions while facilitating.

Try This	Discuss the Challenge Upfront

 Anytime the leader facilitates, but particularly if the issue is a sensitive one, discuss upfront the challenge you, as the leader, face in wearing the two hats of team leader and meeting facilitator. Get input from the group as to how you can best make this work.

Finding a Balance

The importance of a decision and the degree to which the leader needs to participate in the decision-making contributes to the complexity of the challenge. Many times, the leader's greatest concern about facilitating meetings is that he or she will be too directive or shut the group down.

In an effort to be facilitative, leaders frequently don't present their experience and knowledge strongly enough. This may end in people feeling good about the process, but often the decision suffers.

Is the leader bringing essential knowledge and experience to the discussion? If the decision would benefit from the leader's active contribution, invite someone else to facilitate.

Figure 11.3: Can the Leader Effectively Lead the Meeting?

Consider these factors. Is the:

Team Climate	Healthy?..Unhealthy?	
Sensitivity of the Issue	Low? ....High?	
Leadership Style	Facilitative? .... Directive?	

Can the Leader Effectively Lead the Meeting?

Facilitative Style + Healthy Climate + Low Sensitivity	=	Yes
Facilitative Style + Unhealthy Climate + High Sensitivity	=	Risky
Facilitative Style + Healthy Climate + High Sensitivity	=	Yes with strong facilitation skills
Directive Style + Healthy Climate + Low Sensitivity	=	Yes with good facilitation tools
Directive Style + Unhealthy Climate + High Sensitivity	=	No
Directive Style + Healthy Climate + High Sensitivity	=	Risky

Team Members as Meeting Facilitators

Team members, like leaders, also face the challenge of being stakeholders and having to demonstrate objectivity when leading meetings of their own team. They too must be able to step back from team issues and be objective when facilitating team meetings.

Some teams rotate the facilitation of meetings among the members. This has many benefits, including:

- Sharing the load.
- Developing a sense of ownership for meetings.
- Raising the level of importance of meetings in the eyes of the members.
- Giving people the opportunity to develop new skills.

The downside may be:

- Less productive meetings due to lack of facilitation training and experience.
- Unfairly putting members into a role in which they may not be comfortable.

When selecting a member to facilitate a team meeting, consider the following questions:

- Who has the strongest facilitation skills?
- Who has the ability to be most objective?
- Who is most comfortable in the role?
- Who has the least stake in the item under discussion?

Contributing Your Own Ideas

As an inside facilitator, either leader or member, it's important that your contribution not be lost. When contributing your ideas, ideally position them somewhere in the middle. Putting them at the beginning or the very end, combined with your position as facilitator, can give the impression that your ideas are driving the decision.

Try This | The Two Hats

Use the "two hats" technique when facilitating meetings of which you are a leader or team member. When putting out an idea or opinion they signal that they are moving out of the objective facilitator's role by saying "I'm putting my leader's hat back on for a minute."

HOW DO YOU DEVELOP MEETING FACILITATION SKILLS?

Use the Meeting Facilitation Skills Development Plan, Figure 11-4, to analyze your meeting facilitation skills, both strengths and growth opportunities. Carefully evaluate each category. It is useful to get input from people who have observed you in the role of meeting facilitator.

1. **Strengths.** It is important to identify the strengths and skills we presently demonstrate and to remind ourselves of them periodically. Confidence sometimes leads to sloppiness or forgetting to use what we already know.

2. **GOs (Growth Opportunities).** List here the aspects of meeting facilitation with which you feel least confident and the skills that you wish to better understand.

3. **Tools.** Beside each growth opportunity, list the tool you will use to develop each one.

4. **Source.** This could include *On Track*, and a specific page number where the information you will use is found or other sources.

5. **Follow-up Date.** Firm up your plan with a follow-up date when you will review your progress in specific GOs (growth opportunities).

Your goal is to move Growth Opportunities to the Strength column.

It is likely that as you continue to develop your facilitation skills, that you will identify additional GOs that reflect the finer points of facilitation.

Get Feedback

Ask a colleague to observe a meeting you lead and provide that person with the Meeting Facilitation Checklist, (Figure 11-5) and ask them to give you feedback at the end of the meeting. If you

Figure 11.4: Meeting Facilitation Skills Development Plan

Name: _____

Strengths	GO's (Growth Opportunities)	Tools	Source	Follow-up Date

Figure 11.5: The Meeting Facilitation Checklist

Did the meeting facilitator:

- ❑ Clarify the group's objectives?
- ❑ Ensure full participation?
- ❑ Ask open-ended questions?
- ❑ Probe for more information or understanding?
- ❑ Challenge the members' thinking?
- ❑ Create a comfortable environment?
- ❑ Develop Meeting Agreements?
- ❑ Encourage innovative thinking?
- ❑ Use Meeting Agreements effectively?
- ❑ Create an energetic environment?
- ❑ Demonstrate flexibility?
- ❑ Listen actively, e.g. eye contact, nodding?
- ❑ Paraphrase?
- ❑ Invite opposing views?
- ❑ Provide an organized structure?
- ❑ Clarify understanding?
- ❑ Deal effectively with negative behaviors?
- ❑ Do process checks?
- ❑ Check for consensus?
- ❑ Ensure closure and commitment to action?

YOUR NOTES

have a specific behavior that you would like help managing during the meeting, describe it to the coach and determine a signal which the coach will give you if you are slipping. For example, you might be:

- Asking closed rather than open-ended questions.
- Moving too quickly and not allowing sufficient discussion.
- Crossing the process/content line and becoming too involved in the group's decisions.
- Tape a meeting that you facilitate. Review it afterwards, ideally with someone skilled in facilitation but you will benefit greatly even if you view it on your own. Identify your key GOs.
- Attend a Meeting Facilitation Skills Workshop. The practice and coaching opportunities you receive in high quality workshops will ensure a skills development growth spurt.
- Invite members to complete the Meeting Check-Up (Figure 11-7, page 175).

HOW DO YOU ENSURE A "THAT WAS A GREAT MEETING" RESPONSE?

"Not another meeting" has long been a common lament among employees whose experience tells them that too many meetings are a waste of time. Now as workloads and challenges continue to increase, people are more actively resisting meetings by either loudly voicing concerns that at one time might have been quietly mumbled over coffee with co-workers or they are refusing to attend meetings.

When people leave meetings with a "that was a great meeting" response, negative attitudes toward meetings even turn around. People willingly participate in meetings led by meeting facilitators who have a reputation for creating worthwhile meeting experiences.

Great meetings have two components:

1. **They are seen as productive.** Meeting members describe productive meetings as: focussed, on track, on time, fast-paced, no rehashing of old "stuff," met objectives, and things were wrapped up tightly.

2. **They are seen as effective.** Members describe effective meetings this way: good level of discussions, open dis-

cussion, energetic, lots of participation, high quality decisions, and buy-in to the outcomes.

All of the information presented in *On Track* is, of course, dedicated to ensuring you can lead more productive, effective meetings with greater ease.

However, because meeting leaders often find it useful to think about the two components separately, in this section we provide a recap of key strategies and techniques presented earlier plus additional information and hints with regard to productive and effective meetings.

How Do You Increase Meeting Productivity?

1. Be Clear about the Purpose of a Regular Meeting

Meetings that are held regularly often lose their purpose. The purpose is why the group holds this particular meeting. The agenda, if there is one, often contains anything that has come up since the last meeting, rather than those items suited to the purpose of the meeting. If you are leading a meeting that happens regularly, check whether its purpose is clear.

If, for example, the purpose is to focus on a particular project, agenda items should relate to that project unless a conscious decision is made to introduce something else.

If your regular team meetings are general purpose meetings, check the next two sections.

2. Manage the Number of Meetings

Once the purpose is defined, use it to determine whether and how often you need to meet face to face. Ask: "Is it necessary to meet face to face to do this?" and "Is it necessary to meet as often as we do to achieve this?"

Caution	"Everything But the Kitchen Sink" Meetings

Use the stated purpose of the meeting to determine what should be on the agenda. All agenda items should be scrutinized to determine how addressing each item fits into the purpose of the meeting. If it doesn't, it should be addressed elsewhere.

YOUR NOTES

YOUR NOTES

 Handle with Care | Manage, Don't Eliminate

In many team, members are so overburdened with meetings that they too quickly jump to the "We don't need meetings" decision. Meetings are essential to teams. They should not be totally eliminated, but must be better managed.

3. Don't Waste Members' Time

In addition to checking each item against the purpose, ask yourself, "Does this item need to be addressed by the entire team?" Perhaps it affects or requires input from a few team members only. When members feel their time is wasted, it is often because agenda items don't apply to them or how they apply to them hasn't been made clear.

These items may be dealt with in another forum, or left until the end, allowing members who need not be involved to leave.

4. Keep Discussions Focused

Meetings go in circles when members have different understandings of what the group has been brought together to achieve. Clarify the objective in pre-meeting materials and at the beginning of the meeting. Post the group's objective(s). Refer back to the objective if the group discussion begins to stray. You might ask the group, "How is this discussion helping us to reach our objective?" This is usually sufficient to nudge the group back on track.

5. Time Agenda Items

Timing agenda items ensures that you make decisions before the meeting about how much the group can productively address, as discussed in Chapter 1 at page 20.

Use the indicated time on your Vital Agenda as a management tool within the meeting. If an item takes longer than anticipated, this should trigger the question of whether to continue the discussion of the item and drop something else off the agenda; whether to bring the discussion to conclusion quickly; or whether to revisit it at the next meeting.

6. Choose the Right Decision-making Method

Consensus reaching can be time-consuming. Use this method only when consensus will also add value, if, for example, all members have a stake in the decision and the issues are important or sensitive or when consensus is necessary for the buy-in required for the effective implementation of the decision.

Majority votes are effective for simple issues or those for which members do not have strong preferences.

Delegate the decision to a member or small subgroup if they are the experts and the decision does not require the knowledge or experience of the entire group. (See Chapter 2 for more information on decision-making.)

The decision has often been made long before the group stops talking about it. Ensure that members have had sufficient discussion to ensure full understanding and buy-in but don't let excessive discussion take place.

Frequently meeting leaders let the discussion run until a few minutes before the end of the meeting and then quickly capture the decision and bring the group to closure. Instead, as soon as you sense a level of agreement, ask the members, "Have we had sufficient discussion to be able to come to agreement that ... ?"

This allows time to:

- Confirm consensus.
- Identify and agree to action items to take the decision forward.

Checking for closure early can often allow you to shorten the meeting.

7. Avoid Rehashing Delegated Decisions

Too often, groups delegate decisions to an individual or committee and then rework the decision once it is presented to them.

When the group decides to delegate the decision, ask the group to clarify what that means to them. Are they saying:

- You have complete authority to make the decision. Let us know what you have decided; or
- You will develop a recommendation that will come to the larger group for discussion and final decision.

Emphasize that if group members have any input they believe is important to the decision-making process, it should be provided upfront, not when the decisions or recommendations are being presented.

YOUR NOTES

8. Priorize Agenda Items

The criteria for deciding which items are most important include time sensitivity or urgency, as well the importance of the issue. The importance of the issue may affect the amount of time devoted to the item and its place on the agenda. Most important issues should be dealt with early in the meeting for several reasons:

- Should the issue require more discussion than anticipated, the group will not run out of time.
- If the meeting is a lengthy one, the group energy level will be higher earlier in the meeting.
- Should people have to leave the meeting early (not a practice to be encouraged but sometimes unavoidable), the most important topics will have been addressed by the entire group.

Caution	Minor Issues that Become Major Debates

 It is common for groups to get into lengthy discussions about issues on which they have strong opinions but that are not very important relative to other agenda items. One group, for example, spent most of a meeting discussing whether drinking coffee should be allowed at the reception desk and only a few minutes discussing other agenda items including budget and staffing.

How Can You Ensure Meeting Effectiveness?

1. Beginning the Meeting

At the beginning of the meeting, remind the group of the importance of both attention to task (what the group needs to accomplish) and attention to the group process (the way in which members contribute and interact with one another):

- Emphasize that the quality of the group's outcomes are directly related to the quality of the group process.
- Invite members to give examples of behaviors that determine an effective group process.
- Tell the group you will, from time to time, be stopping the group discussions briefly to check with the group on the effectiveness of their process.
- Develop Meeting Agreements (Chapter 1, page 40).

It also can be helpful to invite members to identify Hope Fors and Hope Nots (see Figure 11-6). Hope Fors are comprised of what members hope will happen in the meeting and Hope Nots relate to what they hope will not happen. Some Hope Fors might include:

- That everyone participate.
- We have fun.
- We come up with an excellent solution.
- We reach consensus.

Hope Nots are usually based on the group's knowledge of how they have managed together in the past and what hasn't worked well. They may also be responses they anticipate as a result of the difficulty of the task they are undertaking and the sensitivity of the issue. Some Hope Nots might include:

- Conflict.
- Rehashing old issues.
- Spinning our wheels.
- Running over time.

Brainstorm with the group to complete the first two columns of Figure 11-6 and then develop strategies for ensuring the Hope Fors happen and the Hope Nots don't. The results can be added to or become the group's Meeting Agreements.

2. During the Meeting

Use the group's Meeting Agreements throughout the course of the meeting. As soon as you observe behavior that could hinder meeting effectiveness, refer to the Agreements. Invite the group members to take ownership for the Agreements and to remind each other if there is divergence from them.

Use performance checks, including the process check, logic check, feeling check and creativity check (see Chapter 4).

Assign a member to be the meeting coach. The coach's job is to observe the meeting and to provide feedback. Provide the coach with a copy of the Meeting Check-Up (Figure 11-7) and ask him or her to use it as a guide during the meeting and to be prepared to share their observations.

Invite the group to use the coaching method in either of the following ways:

YOUR NOTES

Figure 11.6: Increasing Meeting Effectiveness

Hope Fors	Hope Nots	Strategies for Ensuring Success

Figure 11.7: The Meeting Check-Up

Rate each of the following statements on a 1 to 4 scale.

1 – We didn't do this at all.

4 – We did this well/consistently.

	1	2	3	4
We:				
• Had full participation.				
• Listened openly to one another.				
• Stretched our thinking.				
• Openly expressed ideas.				
• Openly addressed concerns.				
• Showed energy and enthusiasm.				
• Started and ended on time.				
• Kept discussion on track.				
• Made decisions effectively.				
• Achieved consensus (if aimed for).				
• Felt the meeting time was well spent.				

	1	2	3	4
The Facilitator:				
• Clarified the objective.				
• Used our Working Agreements.				
• Stopped periodically to check our process.				
• Clarified understanding of discussion points (as required).				
• Provided a structure for the decision-making process.				
• Checked for consensus/agreement.				
• Ensured each item was brought to closure with commitments to action.				
• Confirmed next steps.				
• Recapped our outcomes/decisions.				

YOUR NOTES

- The coach may be invited to interrupt the discussion when he or she observes a process issue that could impede the group's effectiveness.
- The coach may provide feedback to the group at the end of the meeting. Providing feedback at the end is useful only if the group will meet again and so can use the information to better their meeting performance.

3. End of the Meeting

Make assessing meeting effectiveness the last agenda item. Ensure that time is booked for this, otherwise members will be doing it hurriedly or not at all before they rush out of the room.

Provide each member with a copy of The Meeting Effectiveness Questionnaire (Figure 11-8) or the very brief Meeting Effectiveness Barometer (Figure 11-9).

You may:

- Ask members to complete the questionnaires and leave them with you. You will review the comments and share them with the group at the beginning of their next meeting (allow five to 10 minutes for its completion).
- Ask members to complete the questionnaire and then discuss their responses at that time. This option requires that the group be prepared to devote 20 to 30 minutes to the discussions.

Congratulate yourselves on your strengths. Discuss the opportunities for improvement. Develop Meeting Agreements based on the opportunities for improvement to ensure that the group uses the information to improve future meetings.

4. Hits and Misses

At the end of the meeting, invite members to discuss the effectiveness of the meeting by identifying the group's Hits — what the group (the members plus yourself) did well in the meeting — and the Misses — what the group could have done more effectively.

See Figure 11-10 for an example of what a list of Hits and Misses might look like. Use the Misses to develop Meeting Agreements to increase the group's effectiveness in their next meeting.

Figure 11.8: Meeting Effectiveness Questionnaire

Answer each question by choosing the descriptive term that applies to your group.

	Never	Occasionally	Usually	Always
Do you have the agenda in sufficient time before the meeting to allow you to prepare?				
In meetings, are members ready to give a report when asked?				
Do members know how to get an item on the agenda?				
Are agendas effectively used, i.e. as tools for preparation for meetings?				
Does each item state what the issue is, and what you want to decide?				
Is there an estimated time alotted for each item?				
Are the items arranged in a logical order?				
Is there time to deal with the entire agenda?				
Are discussion items effectively priorized?				
Are "information only" reports useful?				
Do all members understand the agenda item to be discussed?				
Is there an attempt to see if everyone understands the problem under discussion in the same way?				
Do members come sufficiently prepared to participate effectively?				
Does the group stay on track?				
Do people listen to others' ideas?				
Are people open to changing their minds?				

Figure 11.8: Meeting Effectiveness Questionnaire – continued

	Never	Occasionally	Usually	Always
Does the group get all the facts out before discussing solutions?				
Is there frequent clarification of points?				
Is there periodic recapping to check "where we are"?				
Does the group stay within the allotted time?				
If running overtime on an item, does the group stop to decide "what do we do?" (e.g. Hold the item for future meeting? Continue and drop another item? If so, which item?)				
Is a decision made for each item requiring one?				
Is there general agreement and support for decisions?				
Does everyone know what the decision is?				
Does everyone know who is responsible for acting on the decision?				
Does everyone know how the decision will be put into action?				
Is there an agreed upon system and date for follow-up?				

Figure 11.9: Meeting Effectiveness Barometer

Consider the effectiveness of your meeting by rating each of the following requirements of an effective meeting.

In your meeting did the group:

	Not well 1	2	3	Very well 4
• Clarify objectives				
• Keeping on track (topic and time)				
• Ensuring full participation				
• Clarify points/ideas				
• Recapping and ensuring commitment to action				

Figure 11.10: Hits and Misses

HITS	MISSES
We all participated.	We wandered off track occasionally.
We built on one another's ideas.	We didn't get agreement on the last items.
We stayed on time.	We didn't explore the minority point of view.

The Two Components – Productivity and Effectiveness

Considering meeting success by examining the two separate components – productivity (task orientation) and effectiveness (process orientation) – often helps meeting facilitators quickly enhance the quality of the meetings they lead. A "that was a great meeting" response becomes the norm. It is not unusual to have the people who previously were reluctant to attend meetings ask "When's the next one?"

YOUR NOTES

How Do You Quick Answer?

Ensure Participation?

- Learn about the group's participation style and prepare accordingly (page 147–149).
- Develop a relationship with the group.
- Model openness.
- Warm up the group with meeting energizers.
- Intervene when negative behavior that could stifle participation is demonstrated.
- Keep the group energized (page 150).
- Establish the expectation that members participate.
- Use Generating Ideas Techniques (page 151).
- Develop meeting agreements that support openness and participation (page 151).
- Address perceived repercussions that might inhibit participation.
- Ensure common understanding of the topic or group's objective.
- Develop group's ownership for the process and outcomes (page 152).
- Break out into smaller groups (page 153).
- Be direct in inviting participation (page 154).
- Help people come prepared to participate.
- Acknowledge and build on ideas offered.
- Deal with behaviors that might shut down participation.
- Add lightness (page 156).

Deal With Senior People in Meetings?

- Before the meeting discuss with the senior person the role they will play in the meeting (page 157).
- Coach the leader (page 158).
- Address the issue upfront in the meeting. Identify with the group ways in which a senior person's presence could affect the meeting. Develop meeting agreements that address these possibilities.
- Be assertive. Intervene if the senior person's behavior is negatively impacting the group process.

Use a Timed Agenda?

- Ensure time allocated to items is realistic. Don't overload the agenda.
- If an item requires more time than allotted, stop before you run out of time to decide whether to:
  - Take the additional time required for the item and take something else off the agenda. If so, what will be removed and when will it be dealt with? Or
  - End the discussion of the item at the scheduled time and continue the discussion at a later time, specify when.

How Do You Quick Answer? – continued

Facilitate the Meeting When You Are the Leader or a Member?

- Discuss with the group issues that may arise when a stakeholder facilitates and develops strategies for dealing with them.
- Do a process check during the meeting to ensure the way in which you are leading the meeting is working.
- When putting forward your personal perceptions or ideas, put the group on notice that you are taking off your facilitator's hat.
- When gathering ideas, contribute your own but position them somewhere in the middle (page 164).
- Acknowledge if the strength of your opinion or stake in the issue will prevent you from facilitating objectively and pass the role to someone else.

Develop Meeting Facilitation Skills?

- Use the Meeting Faciliation Skills Development Plan (Figure 11-4).
- Get feedback (page 165).
    - Invite a colleague to observe you and provide feedback.
    - Tape a meeting and review it.
    - Attend a meeting facilitation skills workshop.
    - Ask meeting members to provide feedback using the Meeting Check-up (Figure 11-7).

Increase Meeting Productivity?

- Be clear about the purpose of regular meetings (page 169).
- Manage the number of meetings.
- Clarify objectives.
- Keep discussions focused.
- Time agenda items.
- Choose the right decision-making method (Chapter 2).
- Avoid rehashing delegated decisions (page 171).
- Priorize agenda items.
- If making a consensus decision, develop a back up plan for use in the event consensus is not possible.
- Don't wait until the last minute before checking for agreement.

How Do You Quick Answer? – continued

Ensure Meeting Effectiveness?

- Highlight the importance of the group process in achieving the group's objectives (page 172).
- Discuss hope fors and hope nots (page 173).
- Develop meeting agreements.
- Refer to the meeting agreements throughout the meeting as appropriate.
- Use performance checks — process, creativity, feelings and logic checks (Chapter 4).
- Assign a group member to act as meeting coach (page 173).
- Use decision-making tools that increase the quality of participation and decisions made (Chapter 3).
- Invite the group to assess the meeting effectiveness (page 176).

And So...

Skilled meeting facilitators are alchemists. They spark a process that changes what could be dull and ordinary into something of exceptional value.

In the opening I emphasized the importance of the role of meetings in the success of any organization. Meetings determine the quality of decisions made in an organization and the spirit with which they are embraced and brought to fruition. Meetings have the power to affect how the group and the individuals in the group feel about themselves. Meetings offer the opportunity for dramatic individual and group growth when individuals learn to set aside their personal assumptions and to engage in dialogue. Effective meetings allow ideas to be turned inside out, mixed together, stirred and shaken to create something much greater than any one of the members could have produced on their own.

All of this from simply bringing a group of people and their ideas and knowledge together in a focused process that taps the best of each of the members.

Anyone invited to facilitate a group of people, coming together to accomplish something, is extended both an honor and an opportunity.

It is an honor to be entrusted with something as important as a meeting. (If others don't recognize the honor they are bestowing on you, they will once you have given them a taste of what spectacular meetings can do. Beware – your profile in the organization will soar.)

When you facilitate a meeting that enriches the participants and the organization you have used your talents to make an important contribution. What an opportunity!

Enjoy!

Worksheets

Worksheet 1: Pre-Meeting Steps Checklist

Meeting Objective

I fully understand the objective. ☐

_____

_____

The wording is clear. ☐

_____

_____

The objective is realistic. ☐
_i.e._ • sufficient time
      • participants have the required knowledge/skills/authority

_____

_____

The Right Participants

Is any one (any skill/knowledge) missing? ☐

_____

_____

Is there a rationale for including each meeting member? ☐
_i.e._ each person has something to contribute or something to gain by being there.

_____

_____

Learning About the Group

For Outside Facilitators
Meet with the team leader and/or meeting organizers. ☐

_____

_____

Meet with meeting members. ☐

_____

_____

Worksheet 1: Pre-Meeting Steps Checklist – continued

Attend a meeting of the group. ☐

_____

_____

Collect information via a survey. ☐

_____

_____

Review information and consider potential impact on the meeting. ☐

_____

_____

Inside Facilitator
Review knowledge about the group and the meeting topic and ☐
consider the potential impact on the meeting.

_____

_____

Design the Meeting

Complete:
  The Vital Agenda ☐
      Or
  The Meeting Process Design ☐

Meeting Notification ☐

Meeting Room

  Lighting ☐

  Chairs ☐

  Ease of eye contact ☐

  Temperature control ☐

  Room set-up ☐

Worksheet 2: Team Survey

To _____   Re _____

From _____   Date of Meeting _____

Please respond to the following questions. The information will help me prepare for our meeting.

I do not require your names.

Thanks for your assistance.

Please rate each of the following statements on a scale of 1 to 4. 1—this never describes our meetings; 2—occasionally; 3—usually; 4—always/definitely. Feel free to add comments.

The team has clear goals   1   2   3   4
If rating a 3 or 4, list two goals.

_____

We are a high performance team.   1   2   3   4
If rating a 3 or 4, describe two recent achievements.

_____

Members work well together.   1   2   3   4
Provide an example to support your rating.

_____

Members pull in the same direction.   1   2   3   4
Provide an example to support your rating.

_____

We feel supported by the organization.   1   2   3   4
Provide an example to support your rating.

_____

We are kept well informed.   1   2   3   4
Provide an example to support your rating.

_____

We share information readily with one another.   1   2   3   4
Provide an example to support your rating.

_____

We share knowledge readily with one another.   1   2   3   4
Provide an example to support your rating.

_____

Team members take initiative.   1   2   3   4
Provide an example to support your rating.

_____

Worksheet 3: Information Please

To _____   Re _____

From _____   Date of Meeting _____

The objective of our meeting is _____
_____

Please answer the following questions to assist me in preparing for the meeting.

Thanks for your help.

List the key issues that relate to our objective.

_____

_____

_____

Briefly describe the different perspectives that members hold on key points. Please put an * beside your own perspective.

_____

_____

_____

If you believe we will face any challenges in meeting our objective, please describe them briefly.

_____

_____

_____

If you have identified challenges, how do you believe we can best overcome them?

_____

_____

_____

Worksheet 4: Meeting Style Survey

To _____   Re _____

From _____   Date of Meeting _____

Please respond to the following questions. The information will help me prepare for our meeting.

I do not require your names.

Thanks for your assistance.

Please rate each of the following statements on a scale of 1 to 4. 1—this never describes our meetings; 2—occasionally; 3—usually; 4—always/definitely. Feel free to add comments.

People arrive on time.	1	2	3	4
We have full participation.	1	2	3	4
We have no discussion monopolizers.	1	2	3	4
We have open and honest communication.	1	2	3	4
People are open to new ideas.	1	2	3	4
Discussions stay on track.	1	2	3	4
We manage our time well.	1	2	3	4
We challenge each other's thinking.	1	2	3	4
We introduce creative ideas/solutions.	1	2	3	4
We use effective problem solving and decision making methods.	1	2	3	4
We achieve consensus with ease.	1	2	3	4
Decisions are fully supported by group members.	1	2	3	4
We follow through on commitments made.	1	2	3	4

Other comments _____

_____

_____

Worksheet 5: Working Environment Survey

Usually completed in an interview with team leader(s) or meeting organizers. May be completed by meeting members.

1. How would you rate the climate within the organization?

1	**2**	**3**	**4**
low			high

    _____

    _____

2. Describe any recent events that may be affecting the climate.

    _____

    _____

3. Does your organization have a history of following through on action items that come out of meetings?

1	**2**	**3**	**4**
no			definitely/always

    _____

    _____

4. Describe any recent decisions/changes that have a significant impact on this group who will be meeting.

    _____

    _____

5. Describe any significant organizational changes not listed in 2 or 4.

    _____

    _____

From *On Track* by Leslie Bendaly © 2002, McGraw-Hill Ryerson.

Worksheet 6: The Vital Agenda

Group: _____

Meeting Leader: _____

Time: _____

Date: _____

Item	Owner	For Input, Decision or Information	The Objective	Come Prepared To	Allotted Time	Commitments to Action

Worksheet 7: Meeting Process Design

Group: _____

Meeting Topic: _____

Meeting Leader: _____

Objective: _____

Time	Activity	Materials	Process Notes

Energizer #1

Identify a common expression or phrase that each of these represent.

1.   __TURN__
     HIM

2.   BR
    A
     N
      C
       H

3.   grape   grape
      grape
  grape   grape

4.   __TRAIN__
    NIGHT

5.   DKEEPHERARK

6.   cONCERN

7.   linehe

8.   Y A P

Answers to Energizer #1

1. Turn on him

2. Broken branch

3. Bunch of grapes

4. Overnight train

5. Keep her in the dark

6. Growing concern

7. He is at the end of the line

8. Payback

Energizer #2

Identify a common expression or phrase that each of these represents.

1.
TRHEOUBLE

2.
ESCAPE

3.
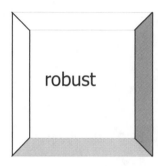

4.
resort   resort   resort   <u>resort</u>

5.
Drunk
clouds   clouds
clouds

6.
$$\frac{Holiday}{c\ c\ c\ c\ c}$$

7.
emotion   emotion
emotion   **emotion**
emotion

8.
millioneon

Answers to Energizer #2

1. He is in trouble

2. Narrow escape

3. A picture of health

4. The last resort

5. High above the clouds

6. Overseas holiday

7. Mixed emotions

8. One in a million

Energizer #3

What do the following words have in common? Example:

camera
dishwasher
gun

Answer: You load them

1. life
    money
    stamps

    _____

2. winner
    pocket
    fight

    _____

3. town
    breakfast
    classes

    _____

4. house
    picture
    nails

    _____

5. worm
    criminal
    subway

    _____

Answers to Energizer #3

1. You save them

2. You pick them

3. You skip them

4. You paint them

5. They go undergraound

Energizer #4

The Problem with Pennies

Materials: ten pennies per group

Instructions:

* Divide participants into groups of approximately six members.

* Present the challenge:

   To change the existing layout of the pennies to form two lines having 6 pennies each.

* Ask the first group that finds the solution to explain it to the others.

Preparation: For each group, arrange ten pennies on a table in the configuration shown below:

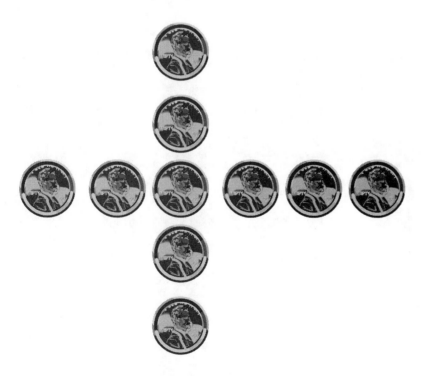

From *On Track* by Leslie Bendaly © 2002, McGraw-Hill Ryerson.

211

Answers to Energizer #4

Solution:

Pick up the penny at the far right and place it on top of the penny in the center.

Worksheet 8: Force Field Analysis

Task

Driving Forces

Restraining Forces

Strategies for Removing Restraining Forces

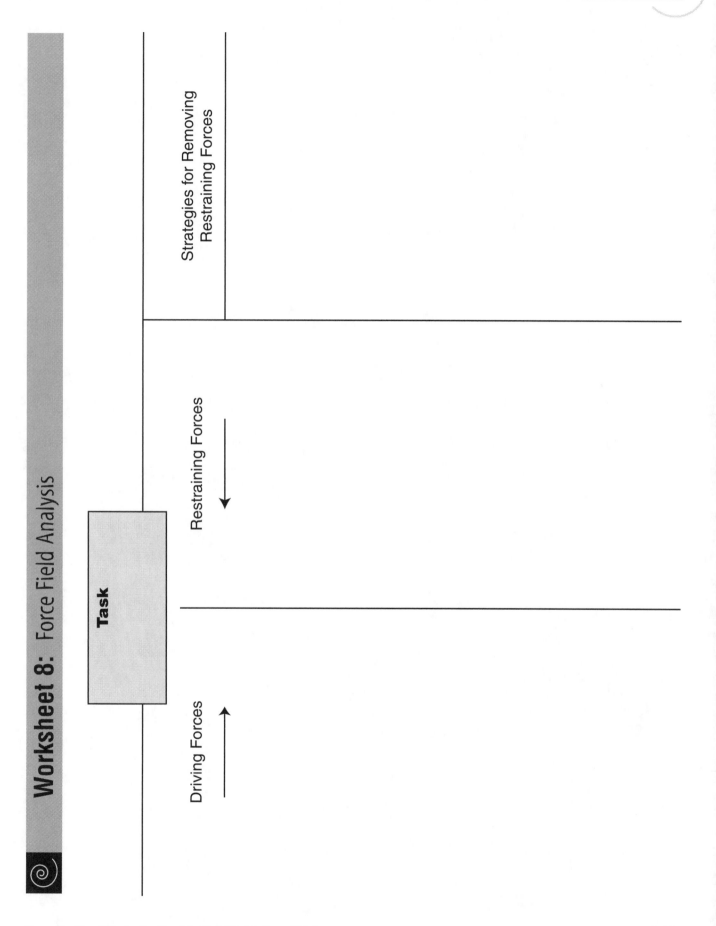

Worksheet 9: Pros and Cons Chart

Proposed Solution	
Pros	**Cons**

Worksheet 10: Decision-Making Criteria Grid

Consider the degree to which each option fulfills each criterion and rate each criterion accordingly on a 1 to 4 scale.

1—Does not meet the criterion at all   2—Somewhat meets the criterion
3—For the most part meets the criterion   4—Fully meets the criterion

Criteria / Options	#1	#2	#3	#4	Total

If some criteria are significantly more important than others, multiply the ratings given them by 2 or 3 accordingly.

Worksheet 11: Build on Common Ground

Option	Benefits	Needs Not Met	Solution that Maintains Benefits & Meets Needs

Worksheet 12: Time for Reflection*

This idea generating process lasts over approximately a four-week period providing time for thoughtful reflection and building on one anothers' ideas.

1. Provide each participant with a notebook in which you have written the problem definition or objective.

2. Instruct each participant to write at least one idea per day in his or her notebook for one week.

3. Provide participants with different color pens or fine line markers. Colors stimulate the creative process.

4. Have participants exchange notebooks at the end of the week. Ask members to use the ideas in the notebook they receive to trigger as many new ideas as possible. The different color ink helps to highlight the building process.

5. Continue the exchange for four weeks, collect the notebooks, summarize and categorize the ideas.

6. Facilitate a group discussion of the ideas that emerge from the process.

* This technique was inspired by the Notebooks technique from *Crunching Creativity* by Michael Michalko.

Worksheet 13: Wordy Brainstorming

1. Describe the problem or objective.

2. Provide the group with a jar full of random words. Put each word on a colored piece of laminated paper. All words should be nouns/objects.

3. Invite the group to draw three or four words.

4. Place each word selected on the top of a flipchart.

5. Invite the group to brainstorm for characteristics of the object. For example, if the word were briefcase, the group might say:

   • It's portable.

   • Comes in different sizes, shapes and materials.

   • It opens.

   • It carries things.

   • It can be locked.

   • There are different styles for different people or uses.

6. Make the connection. Force the group to look for connections between the briefcase and possible solutions to your problem. You might ask, "How is the briefcase like the ideal solution to our problem?" or "Which briefcase characteristic could also be characteristics to the solution of our problem?"

   For example, if the problem is "We can no longer afford to fly all of our sales people to head office for the product launch."

   Perhaps the briefcase characteristic "it's portable" would trigger thinking about taking mini-product launches to each region.

   "There are different styles for different people or uses" might trigger the idea that the mini-launches could be designed to highlight the new product features most important to a particular region.

Worksheet 14: Picture It

1. When problem solving, break the group into smaller work groups — ideally three to six people.

2. Ask that they draw something that reflects the current situation or problem. For example, in a team building session: "Draw an animal that reflects the characteristics of your team today."

   Then ask them to draw the ideal, for example, "Draw an animal that reflects the team you want to be."

3. Invite each group to present their pictures and the characteristics each represents.

4. Examine each characteristic and brainstorm to identify ways to move from the current state to the ideal.

Worksheet 15: Brain Writing

1. Clarify and post the problem or objective.

2. Distribute large index cards.

3. Invite participants to each write an idea on a card and pass the card silently (no discussion) to the person on their right. Ask them to write large enough to be readable from a few feet (cards will eventually be taped on a wall).

4. Instruct the members to read the cards passed to them and write down build-ons or new ideas inspired by them. Allot 20 minutes for this part of the activity.

5. Collect the cards and have group members tape them to a wall.

6. Invite members to gather around the posted cards. Ask the group to look for categories of ideas.

7. Write category headings and stick them to the wall. Move the cards under the appropriate headings.

8. Clarify understanding of the ideas.

9. Distribute colored dots and use the Multi-Voting Technique (page 76) to select the top ideas.

Worksheet 16: Participation Survey

Consider your group's meetings and respond to each of the following statements by rating it on a scale of 1 to 4:

1 – Does not describe us at all.

4 – Describes us all of the time.

#	Statement	1	2	3	4
1.	Everyone participates in our meetings.	1	2	3	4
2.	Some members participate more actively than others.	1	2	3	4
3.	Some members more strongly influence outcomes.	1	2	3	4
4.	We experience conflict in our meetings.	1	2	3	4
5.	We make decisions easily.	1	2	3	4
6.	Members readily raise concerns.	1	2	3	4
7.	Members contribute ideas and solutions.	1	2	3	4
8.	Members receive feedback well.	1	2	3	4
9.	Members give feedback well.	1	2	3	4
10.	Members leave our meetings feeling positive.	1	2	3	4

Worksheet 17: Meeting Facilitation Skills Development Plan

Name: _____

Strengths	GO's (Growth Opportunities)	Tools	Source	Follow-up Date

Worksheet 18: The Meeting Facilitation Checklist

Did the meeting facilitator:

- ❏ Clarify the group's objectives?

- ❏ Ensure full participation?

- ❏ Ask open-ended questions?

- ❏ Probe for more information or understanding?

- ❏ Challenge the members' thinking?

- ❏ Create a comfortable environment?

- ❏ Develop Meeting Agreements?

- ❏ Encourage innovative thinking?

- ❏ Use Meeting Agreements effectively?

- ❏ Create an energetic environment?

- ❏ Demonstrate flexibility?

- ❏ Listen actively, e.g. eye contact, nodding?

- ❏ Paraphrase?

- ❏ Invite opposing views?

- ❏ Provide an organized structure?

- ❏ Clarify understanding?

- ❏ Deal effectively with negative behaviors?

- ❏ Do process checks?

- ❏ Check for consensus?

- ❏ Ensure closure and commitment to action?

From *On Track* by Leslie Bendaly © 2002, McGraw-Hill Ryerson.

Worksheet 19: Increasing Meeting Effectiveness

Hope Fors	Hope Nots	Strategies for Ensuring Success

Worksheet 20: The Meeting Check-Up

Rate each of the following statements on a 1 to 4 scale.

1 – We didn't do this at all.

4 – We did this well/consistently.

	1	2	3	4
We:				
• Had full participation.				
• Listened openly to one another.				
• Stretched our thinking.				
• Openly expressed ideas.				
• Openly addressed concerns.				
• Showed energy and enthusiasm.				
• Started and ended on time.				
• Kept discussion on track.				
• Made decisions effectively.				
• Achieved consensus (if aimed for).				
• Felt the meeting time was well spent.				

	1	2	3	4
The Facilitator:				
• Clarified the objective.				
• Used our Working Agreements.				
• Stopped periodically to check our process.				
• Clarified understanding of discussion points (as required).				
• Provided a structure for the decision-making process.				
• Checked for consensus/agreement.				
• Ensured each item was brought to closure with commitments to action.				
• Confirmed next steps.				
• Recapped our outcomes/decisions.				

Worksheet 21: Meeting Effectiveness Questionnaire

Answer each question by choosing the descriptive term that applies to your group.

	Never	Occasionally	Usually	Always
Do you have the agenda in sufficient time before the meeting to allow you to prepare?				
In meetings, are members ready to give a report when asked?				
Do members know how to get an item on the agenda?				
Are agendas effectively used, i.e. as tools for preparation for meetings?				
Does each item state what the issue is, and what you want to decide?				
Is there an estimated time alotted for each item?				
Are the items arranged in a logical order?				
Is there time to deal with the entire agenda?				
Are discussion items effectively priorized?				
Are "information only" reports useful?				
Do all members understand the agenda item to be discussed?				
Is there an attempt to see if everyone understands the problem under discussion in the same way?				
Do members come sufficiently prepared to participate effectively?				
Does the group stay on track?				
Do people listen to others' ideas?				
Are people open to changing their minds?				

From *On Track* by Leslie Bendaly © 2002, McGraw-Hill Ryerson.

Worksheet 21: Meeting Effectiveness Questionnaire – continued

	Never	Occasionally	Usually	Always
Does the group get all the facts out before discussing solutions?				
Is there frequent clarification of points?				
Is there periodic recapping to check "where we are"?				
Does the group stay within the allotted time?				
If running overtime on an item, does the group stop to decide "what do we do?" (e.g. Hold the item for future meeting? Continue and drop another item? If so, which item?)				
Is a decision made for each item requiring one?				
Is there general agreement and support for decisions?				
Does everyone know what the decision is?				
Does everyone know who is responsible for acting on the decision?				
Does everyone know how the decision will be put into action?				
Is there an agreed upon system and date for follow-up?				

From *On Track* by Leslie Bendaly © 2002, McGraw-Hill Ryerson.

Worksheet 22: Meeting Effectiveness Barometer

Consider the effectiveness of your meeting by rating each of the following requirements of an effective meeting.

In your meeting did the group:

	Not well 1	2	3	Very well 4
• Clarify objectives				
• Keeping on track (topic and time)				
• Ensuring full participation				
• Clarify points/ideas				
• Recapping and ensuring commitment to action				

Index